The Quick Guide to Classroom Management

Richard James Rogers

BSc (Hons), PG Cert Ed (CT),

Cert Maths (Open)

The Quick Guide to Classroom Management/ Richard James Rogers. —1st ed.
ISBN 978-1505701944

Contents

This book is dedicated to every teacher who has found the job to be difficult and stressful. There is light at the end of the tunnel (and it's not an oncoming train!)

ACKNOWLEDGEMENTS

I would like to thank my wife: Mrs Natvaran Rogers, for assisting me in more ways than I can count. This book is just as much your creation as it is mine, as I wouldn't even have got past the first chapter without you. I love you, now and forever. You are an angel that God sent into my life.

Secondly, I would like to thank my parents: Mr Peter Rogers and Mrs Betty Owen. Your guidance during my formative years gave me the tools I needed to progress to my current stage in life.

Thirdly, I would like to thank my former students (who are the illustrators of this book): Miss Suttiya Lertyongphati and Miss Khim Pisessith. You were both among the best students I ever had the pleasure of teaching, and I am so incredibly proud of how you've become the skillful, hard-working and mature young women that you are today. You are both shining examples of what hard-work and motivation during our years at high school and university produces: empowered individuals who are ready to serve society by doing what they love best, and who are always ready to keep on learning as life progresses along its uncertain path.

I would also like to thank a number of former colleagues who have had a particularly positive impact on my professional development over the years. You've made me the teacher I am today:

- Dr John Lewis (My former PGCE tutor at Bangor University). Your care and support through one of the toughest years of my life laid the foundation stones for my career.

- Mr Roy Smithson (Head of Science at St. David's High School, Saltney, England). You were my 'AS' – Level Biology teacher for one year and, later, one of my PGCE mentors. Your overwhelmingly professional conduct at all times sent subliminal cues to me which I only wish I had acted on sooner.

- Mr Paul Graham (Science College Director at Chester Catholic High School). Your sincere praise, at times when I was feeling overwhelmed, motivated me to work hard and succeed.

- Ms Divya Suntewari (My former Head of Science at Traill International School, Bangkok). You were so caring and kind to me, and you gave me the feeling of being trusted and valued. Thanks to you, I thoroughly enjoyed my first job in Thailand.

- Mr Michael Callan (My former Head of Science at St. Andrew's International School, Bangkok). Your direct approach to management ensured that I was always clear about the tasks that were before me.

- The many other colleagues and managers who have helped me along the way. Your interactions with me sculpted the framework of this book.

Miss Khim Pisessith

I am Khim Pisessith, an old student of Mr. Richard Rogers. I recently graduated from Chulalongkorn University, after following the International Program in Design and Architecture (INDA). Drawing is an activity I really enjoy and is a great stress-reliever (I mainly do digital work, but I also love to sketch buildings and landscapes). It was my pleasure to contribute to this book.

Contact: *should_you_wonder@hotmail.com*

Miss Sutthiya Lertyongphati

My name is Sutthiya Lertyongphati or Pop for short. Currently, I am in my final year of pursuing a bachelor's degree in Electronic and Computer Engineering at The University of Nottingham. The assignments and projects at the university are quite difficult and sometimes stressful, so I often spend my leisure time drawing in order to relax. To be assigned to illustrate different tasks is challenging but I still love what I do and if the client is satisfied, then so am I. It was a pleasure for me to have an opportunity to illustrate this book. Some of Mr. Richard's tips I was taught when he was my mentor back in high school also helped me through the course.

Contact: *popslittlespace@gmail.com*

Introduction

Most books about classroom management are filled with tricks and techniques that help the teacher to engage with his or her students in a better way. Like paracetamol for a chronic headache, these books offer a temporary relief for the symptoms of bad teacher-student rapport without addressing the root causes. *The Quick Guide to Classroom Management: 45 Secrets That Every High School Teacher Needs to Know* is not one of those books.

Effective classroom management depends upon how effectively the teacher deals with the dynamic interplay of many factors in the life of the child. This book will teach you, through the hard-earned experience of the author and the contributors, the secrets of:

1. Working effectively with parents: your key customers

2. Enjoying productive relationships with your co-workers

3. Building and maintaining rapport with your students

4. Actively engaging your students in the learning process

5. Engaging your advanced learners (such as your 'A' - Level, SAT and IBDP students)

6. Managing student behaviour in a way that is non-confrontational

7. Using ICT to effectively enhance the learning process

8. Teaching overseas, and the special challenges this involves

It is only when we are able to appreciate how all of our interpersonal interactions affect our students, on a daily basis, that we finally become the unique expert classroom managers that we can be. There is no 'one size fits all' methodology that will transform our daily experiences as teachers. Instead, we have to find the way that works best for us, and this book teaches you exactly how to do just that.

Mr Richard James Rogers

Bangkok, Thailand

October 2015

CHAPTER 1

Building Rapport: Creating a working relationship with your students

> "Building trust, using humour and getting to know the students outside of the classroom can not only help to better understand the background of students but can also help with classroom management and instruction."
>
> **Dr. Olenka Bilash (Professor, Coordinator of Second Languages and International Education, University of Alberta)**

Have you ever noticed that some teachers just seem to be admired and well-liked by their students? Effortlessly, they seem to be able to control behaviour and foster a working relationship with their students. These teachers have effectively used their personalities to generate rapport. Put simply, rapport is a relationship in which the student enjoys working productively with the teacher. It is the single most important facet of a successful educator, and its effectiveness depends upon the character of the teacher and how efficiently this is employed in all interactions with his or her students. Rapport feeds into all of the other aspects of teaching and learning mentioned in this book and, if you master it, your students will benefit immensely and you will find your work as a teacher more rewarding than ever before! Let's start our journey by taking a look at the different elements which constitute this essential feature of outstanding teaching.

Secret number 1: Take a genuine interest in the life of your students

Youth is a time when so many things are happening, both positive and negative. Young people at high school are involved in a range of human-relationship dynamics which involve family, school, friends and the people associated with their hobbies or interests. Humans are full of energy at this time, and the interconnections between the life of a student both inside and outside of the classroom create opportunities for us to channel this energy positively and:

- Build trust

- Use humour within lessons

- Create a sense of importance and empowerment in our students

- Offer guidance and support to students with difficulties

- Create an environment of cooperation and compliance

- Encourage our students to formulate their own learning goals

- Personalise our lessons

Becky was an experienced and well-liked teacher of secondary science. She got on very well with her students, and parents would often mention that they appreciated her 'special attention' to their children. She was liked by her colleagues, and she enjoyed her work. One day, her physics student came to school with a broken arm in a plaster cast. Josh, a keen gymnast, mentioned that he had fallen very hard in a training session two days ago. Becky immediately knew that this was golden information for her lesson planning.

In Josh's next physics lesson, Becky was teaching the class about forces and motion. As Josh entered the class, she presented him with a starter activity revolving around the forces that act upon a gymnast when taking off and landing on a springboard. She also asked Josh how he was doing (and she was sincere in asking). He said he was healing well, and Ms Becky mentioned that "We can use your experience to help the class today, would that be okay?". Josh said "sure". After completing and peer assessing the starter worksheet, Ms Becky asked for Josh to tell the class what had happened to his arm. He gladly told his story, and Ms Becky asked for everyone to clap after he had finished. Using humour and good teaching practice, she said "So using Josh's story to help you, what do you think one of today's objectives could be"? One student mentioned a funny comment about how you should always land on your feet and not on your arm like Josh did, which Ms Becky responded to with a smile and a giggle. After this, and with some prompting from their teacher, some students spoke about the importance of gravity in determining the force upon impact, and the speed of free fall. At the end of a very interesting and varied lesson, Becky allowed her students the opportunity to sign Josh's plaster cast, if they hadn't done so already.

This example demonstrates the power that taking an interest in your students can have on the quality of a lesson. Let's examine what Becky did that made this lesson (and her rapport, or relationship with her students, so special):

- Becky used the hobby of her student to generate a lesson activity (the starter worksheet)

- Becky shows a sincere care and concern for her student

- Becky was genuinely interested in the life of her student outside of the classroom (as she was with all of her students)

- Becky uses student experiences and 'expertise' to enhance the lesson content (she asks Josh to talk to the class about what had happened)

- Becky is tasteful in her humour, and she makes sure that Josh is happy to share his story before she asks him to do so.

- Becky rewarded the class for their good work by allowing them a few minutes at the end to sign Josh's plaster cast. Not only did this subtly reveal her caring and 'human' nature, but it also bonded the class together as a whole.

It was the great John Steinbeck himself who said that *"And, of course, people are only interested in themselves. If a story is not about the hearer he will not listen. And I here make a rule – a great and lasting story is about everyone or it will not last. The strange and foreign is not interesting – only the deeply personal and familiar"*. If you and I are to build positive relationships with our students, then we need to try and make our lessons *deeply personal and familiar*, and show a genuine interest in our students. Building rapport begins and ends with showing a sincere, professional attentiveness to our students and if we are to be good classroom managers, then the first thing we must do is establish a good rapport with our kids.

Secret number 2: Use humour to enhance learning

John's Year 10 English class was generally a cooperative and friendly group of students. One problem persisted though; a problem found in scores of classrooms the world over: low-level disruption. This class was notorious for doing as they were told but having a lack-luster approach to tasks: often chatting when more 'work' should have been done. John, a man from a traditional British family, saw himself as a 'staunch disciplinarian' and he would often respond to chatter and distraction by shouting at the students who he thought were responsible for it. He would hand out scores of detentions, all of which ate into his lunchtimes and his free time after school. Had this have solved things, John might be forgiven for feeling proud of his vigilant approach. However, the problem didn't go away, and students started to resent going to John's lessons and they began to dislike him personally. John had effectively created a very negative environment in the classroom and this was not conducive to effective learning or positive behaviour.

As behaviour got worse and worse, and students felt that they were being treated 'unfairly', John realised that he needed a radically different approach to his teaching methodology. He decided to attend a professional development course in accelerated learning, and after a day of various workshops his eyes were opened dramatically. "I had been making fatal mistakes since I started working with this class" said John. "I hadn't shown them my human side, and I was too quick to criticise. I didn't use my personality to generate humour and I created an environment of negativity".

What do you think John did the next time he heard students chatting in his class? He used humour and his personality to 'lighten the mood' whilst, at the same time, getting the students back on task. "My student, Billy, was chatting to a girl called Sarah when he should have been listening to another student read a Shakespearean sonnet to the class. Normally, I would have responded to this by reading him the riot act and exploding, or putting both students on detention. Knowing that this could cause a backlash, or at least create an unhelpful atmosphere in the class, I decided on a different tactic. I said 'Billy, please stop flirting with Sarah. You can do that at break time' and I smiled. The response I got was a giggle from the class and a bit of teenage awkwardness from Sarah as she said 'Ugh! I don't think so'. After this, everyone listened attentively to the sonnet, and we proceeded on to our group activity".

Use humour to create a lively, relaxed learning environment

John's story demonstrates the power that humour can have in making a lesson more palatable for students, and how humour can be used to keep students on-task. Again, it makes our human nature become visible to our students and, if used tactfully, it can even make lesson content more memorable and can help with behaviour management. You have to be careful though, as some forms of humour will work with some students but not others. You need to have a good knowledge of your class before you employ the tactic that Josh used in the example above. You really need to know your students well, as not every student you have will respond in the same way to the humour that you use.

Humour alert!

- Always make your humour age-appropriate, tasteful and try to stay away from sarcasm: this can be offensive in some situations.

- Don't be artificial: use your own personality to direct the humour of the lesson.

- You need to be able to gauge whether or not your students will respond to the humour positively or negatively

- A joke that works with one student may not work well with another

- Don't be upset if you don't get it right. It takes time and experience to get to know your students and use humour in an appropriate way

I recall teaching a biology lesson some years back in which we were looking at inherited and environmental traits. One girl in the class asked to be excused to use the facilities and upon leaving she said something to her friend and was replied to with the word "retard!". I tackled this in a non-confrontational way by jokingly asking "Is being a retard an environmental or inherited trait" and she said "both!". The whole class giggled, the situation was forgotten about and the students were back on task in a matter of seconds.

In summary, humour increases happiness in the classroom, removes inhibitions, makes the teacher appear more human and can even be used as a behaviour management tool. To add to this, decades of methodical research have shown that humour can even help students remember key concepts for long periods of time, if it is used to illustrate a concept that has just been taught[1].

---

[1] Banas, J. A., Dunbar, N., Rodriguez, D., and Liu, S. (2011). *A review of humor in education settings: Four decades of research*. Communication Education, 60 (1), p.115-144.

Some effective ways to use humour in the classroom

1. Tackle disruption with light-hearted comments that make the students aware that they need to be on task, without being antagonistic. Use knowledge about student interests if possible (e.g. "David, I know you must be talking about the next ramp you're going to fly off on your skateboard, but if you could please listen to me at this moment then I would be most grateful", or "Simone, I'm sure that Diane already knows what a great dancer you are, so if you could please focus on the task in hand, then that would be great"). Remember, students may respond to this so be ready to be light-hearted and direct the conversation back to the task in hand.

2. During group activities or short tasks, you can play some silly music (not too loud) to lighten the mood. You can start by saying something like "I'm going to play everyone's favourite music", and then proceed to play something funny and upbeat.

3. You can sing to your students. That's right, I did just say that! You can make up silly songs about whatever the lesson content is and sing or rap them to the class. You can also get the students to do this too.

4. Use your whole physiology to generate laughter. A laugh eases tension and nurtures creativity. Use changes in your voice, funny personal stories, exaggerated facial expressions, dance moves and anything you can think of to raise a smile and a giggle.

5. Use learning games to make the atmosphere more happy and relaxed. If you're a languages teacher, you may want to make your students formulate silly phrases, or use the vocabulary games mentioned in Chapter 2.

6. Make up rhymes, acronyms and funny mnemonics. For example, MR FAB is an acronym for Mammals, Reptiles, Fish, Amphibians and Birds (vertebrate animals) and "Never Eat Shredded Wheat" is a mnemonic for "North, East, South, West". Even better: get the kids to make up their own.

Secret number 3: Praise and encourage your students regularly

Joanne had recently qualified as a secondary school science teacher and had just started her new teaching post at an English comprehensive school. She was excited about the new challenges she would face, and was ready to put all of her training into action. She had been given responsibility for a Year 11 (age 15 – 16) general science class. Their previous teacher had left her some handover notes, and had specified that she must be careful when dealing with one student in particular: Damon. This young man was notorious for being argumentative, aggressive and non-cooperative. She was told that she must not confront him under any circumstances. Naturally, Joanne was more than a little apprehensive when she met this class for the first time.

Damon walked into the science lab slightly later than the rest of his peers, and Joanne greeted him with a friendly "Welcome in young man, please take a seat". This caused a giggle amongst the rest of the students, who were naturally expecting the same reaction that Damon's other teachers would have given him – a good telling off! Damon sat down as instructed, but, being a feisty young teen ready to push the boundaries and test what he could get away with, he pulled out a can of cola and started to drink it at his desk (something that is generally not allowed in a science lab). Joanne, knowing what she had been told about Damon, decided on a very positive and useful approach: she decided to ignore this misdemeanor at that moment and proceed on with the lesson.

As the lesson proceeded, Joanne set a group work activity and walked around the classroom to see how the students were getting on. As she passed Damon, she noticed that he had a very neat and organized set of felt-tip pens on his desk, arranged in a very nice standalone display case. Joanne praised Damon with a "You're so organised, Damon. It's good to see that you're prepared for your lessons. I wish that every student was as prepared as you are." What do you think Damon's reaction was? - He was absolutely stunned! This was a young kid who was accustomed to being reprimanded, put on detention and confronted on a daily basis. Here was a new teacher who could actually see his worth, and what he could contribute. He lapped up the praise, and responded with an "Umm, err thanks. I always like to be ready for my lessons. I also love art". This led to a short conversation about Damon's love of drawing tattoo designs. Joanne subtly drew his attention to the artistic graphics on the cola can, and reminded him he couldn't drink it in the science lab. He smiled. Later that lesson, Joanne assigned him the role of 'Work Presentation Chief' for the class. Each lesson, from then on in, Joanne made sure that she praised Damon for his work, and allowed him to go around the class and assess the presentation skills of selected students. What was the effect on Damon? - He became Joanne's best student. He felt empowered, because, like all human beings, he craved *a sense of importance* and he craved *appreciation*. When Damon achieved his grade C in GCSE Science that year (a massive accomplishment considering his turbulent history) he said to Joanne "It was all because of you, miss". Even at that moment, Joanne praised him by responding with "You did all the hard work, Damon".

"Any fool can criticize, condemn and complain - and most fools do."

Dale Carnegie (Author of How to Win Friends and Influence People – an international bestseller)

What do most people do when they are criticized? How do most people respond when their character or judgement is scrutinized? Answer: most people try to justify themselves, and this often leads to resentment felt towards the person doing the complaining. Your students are no different in this respect than you or I. We all love to know that we're doing a good job, and we all want to feel appreciated and important. Make your students feel appreciated by praising them often, and make sure you mean what you say!

The Golden Rules of Praise and Encouragement

- Use a variety of methods to praise and encourage your students. Comments written on their work, verbal praise in the classroom, multimedia-based praise (e.g. comments on blogs, stars on student-generated websites, 'stickers' in VLE chat forums, etc.) and informal chats outside of the classroom are all great ways to make your students feel appreciated and important.

- Praise only works if it is sincere. Flattery loses its effect over time. Always find something genuine and meaningful to praise.

- If a student produces a really good piece of work, then make sure you show it to the class as a good example to follow! This will make the student feel extra special, and will encourage both the student and the rest of the class to work even harder. If your school has a VLE, then a novel way to do this would be to scan the work and post it on your subject page. If not, then simply projecting the work onto your interactive whiteboard, or just holding it up in front of the class will have an uplifting effect on that student.

- When you do have to reprimand or correct your students, make sure you praise them for something first. Every human being, no matter who they are, receives criticism much better if their inhibitions are overcome with praise first. A good rule is the "two stars and a wish rule", where you praise two things that went well, and you suggest a target for the future.

Use sincere, meaningful praise to motivate your students. You can always find something to praise a student for.

- Remember to keep praising students who consistently produce good work. These students often get forgotten because they tend to be very compliant and just generally 'get on with it' and offer no problems in terms of behaviour management. It is important to keep encouraging students like this. Praise should not be used exclusively as a motivation tool for underperforming or poorly behaved students.

Secret number 4: Use positive subject-specific feedback on student work

We've touched on this a little bit in the last secret, but here I would like to emphasise the need to offer specific praise that matches the subject being taught. One way of building rapport with students is to generate within them a love of the subject you are teaching, not just a love of your teaching style. Students are much more likely to enjoy the content of a subject if they are rewarded with praise when they meet specific criteria.

Christine was a Year 7 student (aged 11 years) at an international school in Brunei. She was in the school library at lunchtime when she was approached by Rebecca: a PGCE student who was doing a project all about the holistic effects of good marking on a student. Rebecca noticed that Christine had a selection of her notebooks in front of her as she was reading a novel. This seemed like a good opportunity for Rebecca to gain some info for her project.

Rebecca asked to see some of Christine's work and, being a keen and confident student, Christine gladly agreed. The first notebook was a science book, in which the teacher had marked the work with lots of ticks, and had put some brief comments such as 'Well done', 'Very good' and 'nice work'. One piece of work in particular stood out – an elaborate leaflet all about the dangers of smoking to human health, which had clearly took Christine some time to complete. Again, a short comment, 'Great work', and lots of ticks were written on the assignment. When Rebecca asked Christine "Why do think you received this comment", Christine replied with an "I dunno, I guess because it is so neat and I also explained the details really well".

After looking at mathematics and history books which were marked in a similar way to this, Rebecca spotted one that really stood out from the pile! Christine's French book was filled with comments from her friends (peer assessed work), stamps with smiley faces and encouraging phrases such as 'keep it up', and lots of detailed, subject specific comments from her teacher. When Rebecca spotted an 'e-mail to a friend' assignment, which had been printed and glued in her book, it was covered with detailed and positive feedback. Rebecca asked the same question as she did with the science work: "Why do you think you did so well on this piece of work?", to which Christine's eyes lit up! "Well, I'm really proud of this work because I found out how to write 'I look forward to seeing you soon' in French, all by myself, and I started the e-mail correctly by writing 'Dear Serene, It's been a long time since I last saw you'. My teacher said that I had used verbs correctly and that I had learned how to write French letters properly. My only target was to use the correct version of 'I am', because I had mistakenly used 'We are' instead".

Rebecca was astounded. The amount of learning and knowledge retention that had occurred because of that one piece of work was phenomenal. The effort that Christine's French teacher had put in to assessing her work had really paid off; both in terms of how much learning was taking place, and in the effort that Christine was prepared to put in to improve and do her own independent research. Which subject do you suppose was Christine's favourite? It was French, of course. "I just really find the subject interesting and Mr Rossington always gives me good feedback and targets for improvement".

Marking student work: Important tips!

- Always give clear, specific and overwhelmingly positive feedback. Identify one or two targets for improvement, and monitor these as the course progresses.

- When a student reaches a target that you have previously set, acknowledge it with praise!

- You don't have to spend loads of time writing long comments on student work. Whilst specific comments are very beneficial, you can also give verbal feedback and use peer-assessment.

- If you do peer-assess work, then make sure you *always* look over the work yourself afterwards. Students do make mistakes when they mark each other's work, and a comment from the teacher acts as an extra 'seal of approval'.

- ALWAYS make sure that students make corrections to their work after it has been marked. This process is commonly overlooked by many teachers, but it is a vital step in the learning process.

On the next five pages you will see various examples of marking that encourages and empowers students. See if you can identify any of the important pointers listed on the previous page, as you look at this work.

BIOLOGY
HIGHER LEVEL
PAPER 2

Candidate session number

| 0 | 0 | | | | | | |

Wednesday 13 November 2013 (afternoon)

2 hours 15 minutes

Examination code

| 8 | 8 | 1 | 3 | – | 6 | 0 | 0 | 2 |

INSTRUCTIONS TO CANDIDATES

- Write your session number in the boxes above.
- Do not open this examination paper until instructed to do so.
- Section A: answer all questions.
- Section B: answer two questions.
- Write your answers in the boxes provided.
- A calculator is required for this paper.
- The maximum mark for this examination paper is [72 marks].

$\frac{50}{72} = 69\%$

Level 6

Well done! You clearly worked hard to complete this paper. Your answers to section B were particularly impressive.

You should probably review the following topics:

1. Photosynthesis and light absorption (Photosystems I and II)

2. Ecology and evolution.

I also think that trying more data-based questions is important (i.e. the paper 2 question 1)

Keep up the good work!
Mr Richard.

INSTRUCTIONS TO CANDIDATES

- Do not open this examination paper until instructed to do so.
- Answer all the questions.
- For each question, choose the answer you consider to be the best and indicate your choice on the answer sheet provided.
- The maximum mark for this examination paper is *[40 marks]*.

$$\frac{25}{40} = 63\%$$

Level 5

Another good attempt. Well done for getting the scale magnification question correct.

You should probably go over growth curves and global warming (i.e. the ecology and evolution topic).

Keep up the excellent work!

Mr Richard

U 10.1 MEIOSIS

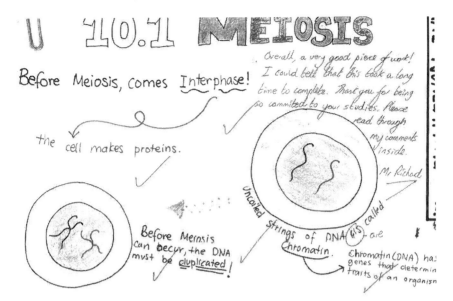

Before Meiosis, comes <u>Interphase!</u>

the cell makes proteins.

Before Meiosis can occur, the DNA must be <u>duplicated</u>!

Uncoiled strings of DNA (His) are called Chromatin.

Chromatin (DNA) has genes that determin traits of an organism

Overall, a very good piece of work! I could tell that this took a long time to complete. Thank you for being so committed to your studies. Please read through my comments inside.

Mr Richard.

There are 4 phrases: Prophase
Metaphase
Anaphase
Telophase.

PROPHASE 1

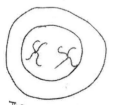 

These chromosomes are called homologou Chromosomes (same size & genes).

sister chromatid.

. The chromosomes condense and become visible
. Chromosomes got packed so they can move easier.

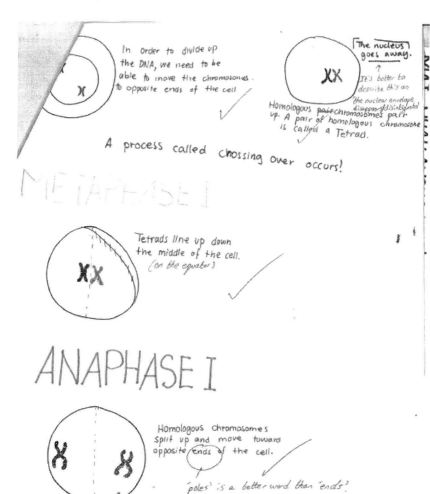

In order to divide up the DNA, we need to be able to move the chromosomes to opposite ends of the cell ✓

The nucleus goes away.

It's better to describe this as the nuclear envelope disappears/disintegrates

Homologous pair chromosomes pair up. A pair of homologous chromosome is called a Tetrad.

A process called chossing over occurs!

METAPHASE I

Tetrads line up down the middle of the cell. (on the equator) ✓

ANAPHASE I

Homologous chromosomes split up and move toward opposite ends of the cell. ✓

"poles" is a better word than "ends"?

Topic 4.2 - Meiosis.

An excellent piece of work which clearly took time to complete. Thank you for putting so much effort into this.
Mr Richards

Meiosis is a reduction division of diploid nucleus to form haploid nuclei.

Homologous chromosomes are two chromosomes that correspond in proportion, value, and structure meaning that they contain the corresponding genes for the same traits.

Homologous pair.

Excellent! I really like how you used the phrase 'reduction division' to describe meiosis. Remember this phrase - it shall prove useful when answering past-exam paper questions on this topic.

THE PROCESS OF MEIOSIS

Meiosis can be divided into two segments, meiosis I and II.

In meiosis I, the chromosomes meet in homologous pairs (synapsis) to create bivalents.

Each chromosome consists of 2 identical 'sister' chromatids, therefore each homologous pair is a group of 4 chromatids, called a tetrad.

The first division occurs by each of these chromosome pairs segregating, or separating onto different sides of the cell.

This produces two cells with the diploid number of chromosomes.

Then, the second division occurs in both new cells when the sister chromatids are separated, pulling apart the chromosome.

This produces four cells with the haploid number of chromosomes.

what is the scientific name for this part?

— Chromosome   — Chromatid.

Good!

Secret number 5: Get involved in the extra-curricular life of your school

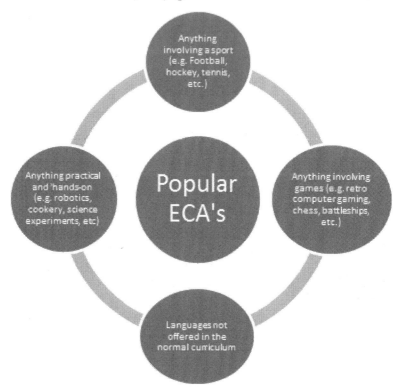

No matter what your background is, you can offer an interesting and high - quality ECA that will benefit your students

Many of your students will have hobbies and interests which go well beyond the scope of the subjects they are studying in school, and which feed into them too. Offering an ECA, or getting involved in one that is already set up, is a great way for you to connect with students and build rapport. In my time as a teacher I've offered ECA's ranging from 'Beginner's German' to 'Code Breaking' and even 'Advanced Mathematics'. Even if you don't have a hobby outside of the workplace, there's still definitely something you can offer. In fact, you may be in a better position this way because you can learn with the students, making you seem approachable, human and open. In order to connect with students we must break down the natural barriers that form between adults and young people, and offering an ECA certainly helps to do this. As an added bonus, you'll get to work with students who you wouldn't normally teach, and this makes you a more 'global' or 'whole-school' figure, which can only add to the connection you make with your students.

Building Rapport: Summary

- Take a genuine interest in your students. Use information about their hobbies, interests and talents to inform lesson planning and the feedback you provide

- Use your personality to generate humour in your lessons. Remember to keep it tasteful, age-appropriate, non-sarcastic and linked to the learning outcomes of the lesson where possible

- Praise your students often, and empower them by recognizing their hidden talents and skills. Remember that praise only works if it is sincere, and remember to keep praising students who consistently work well.

- Use a variety of assessment and marking strategies to give specific feedback to students. Always ensure that students know what they've done well on an assignment, and always provide at least one specific target for improvement. Never outright criticize any student; always mention positives first, and then talk about 'mistakes' as targets for improvement.

- Get involved in the extra-curricular life of the school. There is always something you can offer to enrich the learning of your students.

CHAPTER 2

Active Engagement: Deliver a stimulating and productive lesson, every time!

"A good teacher, like a good entertainer first must hold his audience's attention, then he can teach his lesson."

Dr. John Henrik Clarke (Founder of the African Heritage Studies Association)

My career as a teacher started when I was very young: only fourteen years old! As a Lance Corporal in Britain's Army Cadet Force (a military-based youth club that is similar to a traditional scout troop), I was responsible for training new recruits in my platoon. I would teach them first aid, map-reading, field craft, weapons-handling, military drill and anything else that was on the training programme. This initial (and unorthodox) introduction to teaching really excited me. I loved demonstrating my skills to the new recruits, and then seeing them apply what I'd taught them correctly. It felt good to be a part of their army cadet 'careers', but it took some readjustment of my personality and some real guidance from the senior officers above me before I became, what I would deem, 'good' at teaching.

The recruits in my platoon, just like the students that populate our classrooms today, wanted something *different*. Since I taught in the evenings, often after the new 'squadies' had been in school all day, I had to come up with teaching strategies that were different to what these kids were getting in their standard school curriculum. This led me on a quest to find out what it is that makes students 'tick'. I was curious about what was needed to make a lesson 'excellent'. How can we make our lessons fun and productive each and every time? Well, on this journey I've identified ten key features that I believe all outstanding lessons need to have (in no particular order):

The ten key features of all outstanding lessons

1. The teacher needs to have a lot of energy, and must sincerely *enjoy* teaching the students in his or her class

2. Each lesson must begin promptly (i.e. as soon as the students enter your classroom, or as soon as the lesson is supposed to start)

3. There must be a variety of different activities present in the lesson (but not too many, as students need time to process information and construct ideas)

4. There must be a review at the end of the lesson, which can be student-generated or teacher-led

5. The lesson must have a clear purpose (or set of 'outcomes'), and the students need to know what these are. The students should also know how they are going to meet those outcomes (i.e. the success criteria).

6. ICT is incorporated in some way to enhance the learning process (this is becoming more and more essential as each academic year passes and, in my honest opinion, I feel that ICT will be the central medium of lesson delivery in all subjects, in most developed schools, within five years of this book being published. Chapter 5 is dedicated exclusively to this topic).

7. The teacher should know the students well, and should have a good rapport with them (Chapter 1 goes into more detail about this)

8. A suitable level of challenge, for all students in the class, must be present. This is often achieved in activities where students have to 'figure things out' for themselves.

9. Assessment of skills and knowledge should take place and the students need to be actively involved in this assessment process

10. Effective collaborative learning must take place with students being involved in a range of creative group activities

You may agree or disagree with some of the items in this list. That's absolutely fine! As 'reflective practitioners' we should be constantly reviewing pedagogy and the way in which we deliver subject content. What I can tell you though is that after 16 years of teaching in a variety of settings, ranging from being an army cadet instructor to teaching differential calculus to IB students, the best results have always come when the above ten principles are applied. What do I mean by best results? - When feedback from inspectors, observers and students is overwhelmingly positive, and when students show a measured *increase in progress.*

If you've been teaching for even a couple of years you'll probably have received training in lesson planning and the techniques needed to engage students. However, the problem with a lot of training programmes (and there are a lot of good ones out there), is that they don't always address the following fundamental issue:

> *"To prescribe a formula for outstanding lessons is to ignore the fact that what makes one lesson outstanding might not necessarily do the same for another, and what works for one teacher with one class might not work for another teacher and another class"*
>
> **Matt Bromley (Educational writer, lecturer and consultant head-teacher)**

Every teacher is different; we all have different personalities, different ways of using our physiology and we all have different ideas. What separates the outstanding educators from the rest is *how effectively they use their personalities, physiology and ideas in their roles as teachers, and how they adapt to suit the needs of different classes.*

My aim for this chapter is to show you some of the ways in which I and the many colleagues I've been privileged to work with over the years have adapted the ten key principles to our lessons, making learning engaging and memorable for our students. I'll start this journey with you by displaying an excerpt from the 'SecEd Guide to What Makes an Outstanding Lesson', as we'll be using this as a point of reference throughout this chapter.

How can you be outstanding?

Pupils

- Rapid and sustained progress for almost all.
- An environment where students learn exceptionally well.
- High levels of engagement, interest, resilience, confidence, independence, courtesy, collaboration and co-operation.

Assessment

- Assessment of prior learning is systematic and accurate.
- During lessons, understanding is checked systematically and effectively, anticipating interventions.
- Appropriate homework is set regularly to contribute to pupils' learning.
- Marking and feedback are high-quality and frequent so pupils know how to progress.

Teaching

- Teachers have excellent knowledge and understanding of their subject.
- Teacher lesson-planning is astute.

- Time is used very well; tasks are challenging and match pupils' needs accurately.
- Activities are imaginative and well-judged to meet the content of the lesson.
- Expectations are consistently high of all pupils.
- Interventions are sharply focused and timely, and match individual needs accurately.
- Every opportunity is taken to develop reading, writing, communication and mathematics skills.

Behaviour and safety

- Lessons proceed without interruption.
- Pupils make every effort to ensure that their classmates thrive and learn.
- There is an atmosphere of respect and dignity in the classroom.
- Behaviour management is systematic and consistently applied.
- Pupils understand unsafe situations and are highly aware of how to keep themselves and others safe.

Checklist by education consultant Tony Thornley

Tony Thornley's excellent checklist on how you can be an outstanding educator. Courtesy of the 'SecEd Guide to ... What makes an outstanding lesson?', in association with ASCL. Published June 2012.

Secret number 6: A prompt start primes your students for learning

As a 17 year old 'A' – Level student at a Roman Catholic school in North Wales, I was a typical lovesick teenager. I was easily distracted, and if I got the chance to slack-off, I was sure to take it! I look back at those days and, to my embarrassment, I sometimes have to cringe! However, one question does come to mind quite often – which lessons were the most productive for me, at a time when my human nature (and my attitude) led me to be quite a disillusioned and lazy teenager? The answer:

it was always, without exception, those lessons that began promptly and had a definite focus.

As teachers we're always very, very busy. There's so much to do in such a small amount of time, and it can be tempting for us to take a rest whilst we're working. Whilst a relaxed environment is generally conducive to the learning process, there is a danger that we can cross the line and create an atmosphere that's too relaxed: one that encourages our students to be unproductive. To illustrate this I can use an example from my personal journey. Perhaps you have had a similar experience?

As a pre-university student all those years ago, I remember some of my chemistry and biology lessons particularly well, but for all the wrong reasons. These lessons would typically begin by the teacher having a nice, casual chat with all of the students in order to create a 'relaxed feel'. Sometimes we would even begin by making a cup of tea for each other before we began, and this made myself and my peers feel 'adult' and 'special', reinforcing the fact that we were the big kids in the school and we had a certain status. This ritual would sometimes last for 15-20 minutes before any real learning took place, with one of my teachers in particular discussing anything that came into mind, whether it was a story from her past or an incident she had had with another pupil. After this long 'introduction', in which approximately a quarter of the lesson had been eaten up, we would begin the lesson properly. But were we motivated at this stage? How had this casual entry into the lesson content affected our ability to learn thereafter? The answer is that for many of us it had generated a lazy frame of mind, and it was difficult to come out of a relaxed state and go straight into a learning activity (which was often rushed, because of the time wasted at the start of the lesson). Charles J. Givens, author and once a multi-million dollar business owner, summarizes this problem very eloquently:

"Success requires first expending ten units of effort to produce one unit of results. Your momentum will then produce ten units of results with each unit of effort."

Charles J. Givens (Author of Wealth Without Risk and Financial Self Defense)

From this we're able to understand that for students to achieve results, they need to gain momentum within the lesson. This adds credence to Tony Thornley's point (from the checklist) that time must be "used very well" and that lessons must "proceed without interruption". However, momentum can only be achieved if the teacher initiates it with an appropriate starter activity that requires at least some effort. So, as soon as the lesson starts (or better: as soon as the kids walk through the classroom door) give your students something to do! This can be:

- A quick quiz or worksheet (requiring around five minutes to complete)

- A question written on the board that the students have to answer

- A quick vocabulary game (more on games in the next section)

- An ICT based task (e.g. using iPads to find out how Oliver Cromwell died, completing an online quiz about dinosaurs or writing a short blog post)

- A role-play or conversation starter with students working in small groups (particularly good for language classes)

- A practical construction activity (e.g. 'Use the coins to make fifty five pence', or 'Use the molecular modeling kits to make a molecule of glucose')

- Cut and stick activities (e.g. matching words to descriptions, adding labels to diagrams, making pictures out of shapes, etc.)

- Surprise scenarios (e.g. turning your classroom into a 'crime scene', and getting your students to take samples and follow clues)

- A treasure hunt (these are particularly good fun, and are also a great way to build ICT into your lessons too).

Do you include an interesting starter activity at the beginning of each of your lessons?

I'm sure that you'll probably have other ideas to add to this list too, and that's fantastic! If not, then don't worry; formulating quick and productive starter activities is a learning process but the good news is, the more you do it, the more ideas you'll have! Remember: after the starter activity has finished, always review what was done. Get the students to mark each other's quizzes, or comment on each other's blog posts, or whatever assessment method you feel is appropriate for the activity. Once that's been done, you can move on to the next crucial step in the teaching and learning process: *defining the learning outcomes.*

Secret number 7: Learning outcomes are most useful when the students have figured them out by themselves

As a very keen and determined PGCE student at Bangor University's outstanding School of Education, I was introduced very quickly to the importance of making my students fully aware of the learning outcomes (sometimes referred to as 'aims' or 'objectives'), every single lesson. On a very fresh summer morning at the beautiful science labs at Bangor's 'Normal Site', I and the rest of the science students were given a deck of playing cards. We were then asked to shuffle them and play poker, but keep any diamonds that were dealt to us, indefinitely. When this was finished, we repeated the game, but this time we kept any multiples of three. Once this was over, we were each given a set of coins and asked to toss each one in turn. If we got a head, we could keep the coin; whereas a tails meant that we had to dispose of that coin and place it into a big tub in the middle of the room. After about 30 minutes of doing this, we started to look at each other with rather puzzled and bemused faces. Some of my friends started to utter "What's the point in this?" and "Why the hell are we doing this?" At this stage, our instructor stopped the activities and asked us all a very simple question: "How was that?"

The replies came slowly at first, but as soon as a few people had mustered enough nerve to reply, more answers soon followed."It was okay, but I wasn't sure why we were playing those games", "It was good at first, but I lost focus after a while" and "The whole lesson just seemed completely pointless". After the exchange of a few giggles, we could all see that this was part of the instructor's plan all along (he was always very shrewd in the way that he introduced us to key concepts). He then asked "What do you think the purpose of this lesson was?". Again, the replies came in thick and fast "Something to do with data and numbers", "Learning how to use games to entertain students" and, finally, one student hit the proverbial nail on the head – "To understand that if the students don't know why they are doing something, then they'll lose focus". This final reply was correct, but incomplete. For this particular session, the instructor was trying to teach us two things. The first objective was to learn that it is easy to 'cherry-pick' data in scientific experiments (hence the collection of the 'diamond cards' and disposing of each coin that had yielded a tails). The second was the one that's most important to me and you: that ***learning is only productive and effective if the students know what the mission or objective of each lesson is.***

Are your lessons simply 'different versions of a computer game with the same exact layout, just different colours and different bad guys to fight'?

After learning this crucial lesson, I quickly put it into practice during my first year of teaching. I would always write the lesson objectives on the whiteboard (or project them on a screen), straight after I had given my starter activity. My lessons always started promptly, and my students always knew what my mission was. However, despite this, something was still missing. The problem was that almost every teacher in my school had been trained in a similar methodology, and were all doing the same thing. Each lesson to my students seemed like, in the words of one Year 9 boy, "different versions of a computer game with the same exact layout, just different colours and different bad guys to fight" (I thought that was quite a profound conclusion, actually. I gave that boy a house point for his linguistic creativity).

So what was missing? Why, despite following best practice, were some of my students still losing focus? Why was it that at the end of each lesson some students couldn't even remember the objectives I'd shown them 45 minutes earlier? Well, the answer, as I discovered much later than I probably should have, was found in that unusual session back at Bangor University. The reason that I can remember that particular lesson so well is because it contained a sense of mystery, and because I and my peers **had to figure out the lesson objectives for ourselves**. But how did we figure out those objectives? Answer: *The activities of the lesson aroused within us a sense of curiosity about its purpose.*

We all remember things better if we've had to discover them by ourselves, as opposed to being 'spoon-fed' the information. More often than not, we are also more proud of those things that we've had to overcome, adapt to and solve by ourselves, than those things we've attained easily, and this principle feeds directly into this very effective methodology for beginning a lesson:

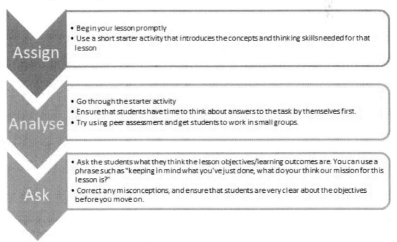

Use the 'three A's' when beginning every lesson. Assign, Analyse and Ask.

By using this methodology you will not only capture your students' attention as soon as the lesson starts, but you will also be encouraging them to use 'higher order thinking skills', especially if the students do the following:

- Build models or construct some kind of concept illustration

- Solve an open-ended problem (e.g. "You have five minutes to build a useful object out of the drinking straws on your desk")

- Include emotion in their work (e.g. "Imagine you are Neil Armstrong on the day he landed on the moon. Write a quick diary entry for him on that day. How did he feel?")

- Solve a logic problem (e.g. breaking a code, or answering a series of questions in sequence which lead the students to a final conclusion)

- Use their physiology in an unusual way (e.g. "You have five minutes to build a tower out of the objects on your desks. One person in your group needs to balance the objects on their head. Who will create the tallest, most balanced tower?")

- Have a choice over whether to tackle the problem using a left or right-brain approach (e.g. "Sarah needs to buy food and drink for a birthday party. In front of you is a price list for every item at Partylicious candy store. Sarah only has 45 pounds to spend, so help her out! Maybe you could write some selected shopping lists for her, or draw a collection of items that she could buy.")

Which of Tony Thornley's boxes does this tick? Quite a few, actually. By beginning our lessons with a creative starter that gets students thinking about the learning outcomes, we're encouraging "high levels of engagement", "assessing prior learning", using time "very well" and using activities which are "imaginative and well-judged". So, start your lessons promptly by assigning a good-quality starter activity, analyzing it thereafter and then asking the students to consider what the objectives of the lesson might be. I assure you, by starting your lessons in this way your students will benefit far more than if your lesson has an unfocussed start, directed solely by the teacher.

Secret number 8: Play games with your students

Go back to the days when you were at school. Pick any class or year group that you were a part of and try, if you can, to remember something about at least one lesson that you had at that time. Maybe it was the grade four art class when you submerged paper in a variety of inks to create a 'marbling' effect for the first time, or maybe it was that geography lesson when you went to visit your local power station. Most people who perform this kind of visualization remember lessons in which either one or more of the following features were present:

1. You were praised for something you did, and you felt proud of your accomplishment (this is actually really important, and is covered in more detail in chapters 1 and 3)

2. You did a fun hands-on activity, such as dissecting a pig's kidney or playing an exciting game

3. Something funny happened to either yourself, your friends or the teacher

4. There was a sudden surprise, such as the fire alarm going off or the teacher dressing up as a famous person in history

5. You were severely scolded for something

6. You figured something out for the first time, and you felt proud of that

7. You saw, heard, tasted, smelt or touched something unusual

8. You suddenly had to get out of your seat and do some funny body movements

9. You did something embarrassing

10. You particularly liked the personality of your teacher, and just simply enjoyed being in his or her presence

As you can see from this list, some items lie more towards the positive end of the 'memorable spectrum' whereas others are more negative and we remember them simply because they made us feel bad. It goes without saying, but as teachers we should definitely be utilizing the positive primers of memory when we are choosing activities for our classes to complete, and one of the most effective of these 'primers' are *games*.

Before we begin looking at some effective games that can be applied to a variety of different subject areas, we need to first define what a game actually is. Whether it's a computer game, an hour of Cluedo™, playing football or memorizing a sequence of words, a game can be defined as follows:

A fun way to solve a problem; often involving competition and some kind of reward system upon completion

The reason I've made a particular point of emphasising this is that in order for you to constantly evolve in your practice, you'll have to invent your own games or modify existing games on a regular basis. This ensures that students maintain a long-term interest in your subject area (or at least look forward to coming to your lessons each and every time). Make sure that there is always some element of competition present. You can play off boys against girls, different tutor groups or house groups or you can simply split the class into equally sized groups, and get the students to come up with their own team names (students love doing this!). Additionally, don't forget to build in some kind of reward. Perhaps the winning team could get two chocolates each, or perhaps you could use your school's existing reward system (e.g. by using 'house points' or 'merits' or whichever systems your school already has in place).

Games can be used:

- At the beginning of a lesson as a starter activity (but make sure they begin promptly. This usually works best if the students already know the rules of the game before the lesson starts).

- To introduce a new concept

- To review concepts at any point in the lesson

- As a fun and effective plenary

- To help EAL students remember key vocabulary

Looking back at Tony Thornley's list, we can see that effective games contribute to high levels of 'pupil engagement, interest and collaboration', along with providing a quick and fun way for the teacher to check progress "systematically and effectively". Games also satisfy the 'teaching' areas of the checklist by proving to inspectors and observers that lesson planning is "astute", providing activities that are "imaginative and well-judged to meet the content of the lesson". In terms of behaviour management (covered in more detail in Chapter 3), games which involve a strong competitive element can create an atmosphere where "pupils make every effort to ensure that their classmates thrive and learn".

I shall now talk you through some of the games that I have used in my time as an educator. Games can be applied to a wide variety of subject areas, and I have personally used them to reinforce concepts in science, mathematics, German, English and even substitute lessons for geography, history, ICT and art. As you read through these examples you should reflect upon how you could use each game in your subject area. You may wish to note down your reflections somewhere.

BINGO !!

This takes some time to prepare, but it is a lot of fun and if you're organised, you can keep the resources to used again and again in the future.

STEP 1: Create a class set of bingo cards that each have possible answers to questions on them (or, to save time, provide blank grids for the students to write answer into).

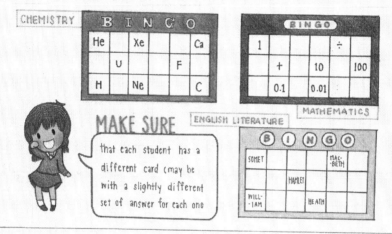

MAKE SURE that each student has a different card (may be with a slightly different set of answer for each one

STEP 2: Play bingo, but don't call out the answers randomly. Instead call out random questions. (the answer to which are on the bingo card.)

How many electrons in a Hydrogen (H) atom?

hmm..

TO AVOID THE GAME GOING ON AND ON FOREVER!!

TIP!

This is a good idea for the teacher to have all of the cards in front of her too, so that she can choose a winner before the game begins.

CORNERS

STUDENTS ARE LINE UP ALONG THE WALL / EDGES OF THE CLASSROOM.

STEP 1: Get all of the students to line up along the walls of the classroom. The teacher must be able to see them.

STEP 2: Ask a question, then say "1.. 2.. 3..." The first student to put their hand up at the count of three get the chance to answer the question.

STEP 3: If the student answer CORRECTLY then, they choose a friend to ELIMINATE / SIT DOWN. The winner student the moves to the same physical position as the losing student.

SCENARIO: John answer correctly and choose Phillip to sit down. John walks to Phillip old position.

JOHN IS CORRECT!

WHY ME?

I CHOOSE PHILLIP!!

PHILLIP   JOHN

The students who are out can answer the question, but they are not allowed to stand up again.

PHILLIP'S OLD POSITION

↑
PHILLIP SAT DOWN

THE OVERALL WINNER OF THE GAME IS THE LAST STUDENT STANDING UP!

A HUMAN GRAPH

Find out how many of your students know the CORRECT ANSWER, or have a certain opinion. Choose a position for each answer, and which the students line up and a human graph is created!!

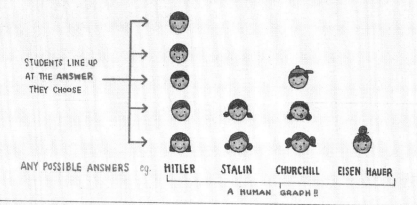

TRUE OR FALSE?

Very simple. Choose one end of the classroom to be the "TRUE" end, and one to be the "FALSE" end. Choose the middle to be the starting point and the position for students who are "NOT SURE."

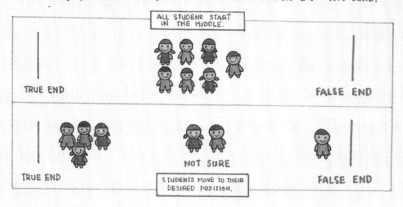

ACTIVITY THAT GET STUDENTS MOVING
HUMAN NUMBERS

If your answers are numerical then get your kids to make number shapes with their bodies!

EXAMPLE:

EXAMPLE:

1.	How many wives did Henry VIII have in total?	
	ANS PICTURE NUMBER	
2.	How many atoms are there in one molecule of CaCO₃?	
	ANS PICTURE NUMBER	
3.	Was ist 'acht' auf Englisch bitte?	
	ANS PICTURE NUMBER	

MEMORY MIND BENDER

This is a simple game but is a lot of fun. It is also a quick intense way to get the whole class to remember lots of key facts.

STEP 1: Get the student to sit in a circle.

STEP 2: Number the students "ONE, TWO, THREE..."

STEP 3: Student number ONE has to say a word or phrase plus a description.

STEP 4: Student number TWO has to say student number ONE's phrase plus one of their own.

STEP 5: This continues in sequence. It gets quite fun when student number 18, has to remember the previous 17 response.

MYSTERY PICTURES

This is a very simple game that forces discovery and knowledge retention. Here's how it goes...

STEP 1: LEADER!

Choose ONE PERSON in your class to be the "LEADER"

STEP 2:

Give the "LEADER" a picture to memorise

↳ that relates to the topic you're teaching

(The rest of the class must not see the picture)

* How a good picture for biology would be :)

STEP 3:

The LEADER must now turn the picture upside down (so that he can't see it) and then describe the picture to the class.

WRONG
Draw DNA molecule

BETTER!
Draw two wavy lines that cross each other often..

umm...

STEP 4:

hmm...

The students must draw what the LEADER has told them to draw.

STEP 5:

um.. what did I just saw...

AHA!!
— I knew it!!

When the LEADER has finished, the students can perfect their drawing by walking over to the original LEADER's picture to see it. The students are not allowed to bring their pictures with them. This forces them to memorise their drawings.

MYSTERY WORD

STEP 1: Write some key words on small pieces of paper. Fold these up and place them in a cup, tin or beaker.

  OR OR

STEP 2: Choose a student to start the game.

ME?
YEP!

STEP 3: The student picks a word from the beaker. The student must not show this word to the rest of the class.

STEP 4: The student gives a clue to the rest of the class, without saying the word that is written on her paper.

First element in the periodic table

The lightest element on the periodic table

hmm..

STEP 5: The students put up their hands to guess what the mystery word is. If a student guesses correctly, they now come to choose a word, and the process starts again.

HYDROGEN!!

let's see...

CORRECT!

The teacher doesn't have to record anything with this game. However, you might want to recognise individual students who recognise multiple words correctly.

THE POSTER GAME

This game is a tremendous amount of fun and it offers you the flexibility to build in lots of ICT and competition.

STEP 1: Split your students into groups of THREE FOUR or FIVE.

STEP 2: Make sure that each student in each group has a number starting sequence from NUMBER 1

"GROUP 1"

"GROUP 2"

20-30 MIN IS OFTEN ENOUGH

STEP 3: the spare colour will be used later

Give each group a different COLOURED PIECE OF LARGE POSTER PAPER, make sure you have a spare one for each group

STEP 4:

Give each group some different information about the topic they're studying. Give each group enough time to make a detailed poster. Make sure you assign roles. EX: student no.1 does the title and student no.2 research with ipad.

STEP 5:

Optional alternative to STEP 4. You can use ICT to get the students to gather the information they need. eg: by doing a QR code treasure hunt.

STEP 6:

ex: stick on the back of a wheelie whiteboard

When the time is up, collect the poster in and stick them up in a place that the student cannot see.

The idea is that when a student hears their number, they will run to the back of the whiteboard (or the place where the posters are) and try to remember as much of the poster they are copying as they can.

(so if a group has a blank piece of PINK PAPER in front of them, then they are copying the GREEN POSTER.

students returning to their group need to tell their group member what to draw or write.

The game ends when the teacher decides that each group has had enough time to copy the opposing group poster.

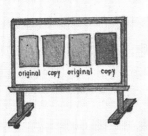

Extra humour is added when the teacher puts all the posters together to compare the ORIGINALS with the COPIES. This often causes a lot of laughter, and the teacher is free to judge which group she feels copied the poster the best.

SNAKE OR BREAK‼

STEP 1: Line the students up. This is THE SNAKE. Make sure they're face forward.

STEP 2: Ask the FIRST STUDENT in the line a question.

STEP 3: If the student answers CORRECTY, then they get to sit down and have a break.

If they answer **INCORRECTLY**, or don't know, then offer the question to another person in the line.

STEP 4: If the student at the front gets the question **WRONG**, then they have to go to the back of the line.

STEP 5: Student who sat down can also answer, but they can't join the line again.

THE GAME ENDS WHEN EVERY STUDENT IS SAT DOWN

SPLAT

STEP 1: Write some key words on the white board.

STEP 2 : Split the class into two teams. The student can choose a team name if they wish.

STEP 3: Choose one person from each team to start the game. They must stand at either side of the whiteboard and face the class.

STEP 4: Say the CLUE for the word and then say "1,2,3". At the sound of 3, the student need to turn around and splat the correct word with their hands.

STEP 5: The first student to **SPLAT** the correct word is the winner. The losing student sits down, and the winning student picks a new person to stand up and fight with him!!

STEP 6: The game continues until all of the words have been 'SPLAT'. The teacher should keep a running tally of the scores for each team and announce the winner at the end.

VOCABULARY MUSICAL CHAIR

STEP 1:

Put all of the chairs in the middle of the classroom. Make sure that the number of the chair is ONE LESS THAN the number of the student. Get the students to stand far away from the chairs.

STEP 2:

What is the slope on a right-angled triangle called? TRIGONOMETRY, PYTHAGORUS, ACUTE, OBTUSE, HYPOTENUSE, REFLEX...

The teacher now asks a question, and then offers a number of different answers.

STEP 3:

HYPOTENUSE

my chair!!

mine!

When the student hear the CORRECT WORD, they run to sit on a chair. Becareful of trips and falls, make sure your students have a clear path to run to the chairs that is free of obstacle.

STEP 4:

LAST ROUND!

YEP!

The process is repeated with one chair being removed each time. Students who are can sit in another part of the classroom. At the end of the game, there should be two students left with only one chair to sit on. The student who sits on this chair first is "THE WINNER!!"

WHO AM I ?

STEP 1:

Write key words, phrases or numbers on the STICKY NOTES.

STEP 2:

Stick the STICKY NOTES on your students head. This game works well if the kids are sat in circle.

STEP 3:

Go around the circle, student by student. The other students have to give clue so that the chosen student can guess what is written on their heads.

STEP 4:

The game ends when every student has guessed what's on their heads.

Secret number 9: Use movement and action to enhance learning

The high school science teacher turns his students into 'electrons' and gets them to walk along a prescribed route in the classroom, reinforcing concepts associated with circuit diagrams and electricity. The primary school mathematics teacher gets her students to make funny shapes with their bodies that represent the numbers 0 – 9, creating a fun way to tackle mental arithmetic problems. The ICT teacher creates a variety of 'human graphs', getting students to line up in columns based upon their chosen answers to assigned questions. What do all of these examples have in common? The students are using movement to solve problems and, in doing so, are engaging *multiple regions of the brain*.

Every single day, our experience of the world around us is created by five main sensations or *senses*, namely:

1. *Touch*: Experiencing the texture of different objects

2. *Taste*: Stimulation of various taste receptors on the tongue

3. *Smell*: Linked strongly with taste and involves stimulation of olfactory receptors in the nasal passage

4. *Sight*: Our perception of light energy through stimulation of cells in the retina

5. *Hearing*: The way in which we receive and process longitudinal vibrational energy

The above five senses allow us to perceive the world around us so that we can make decisions effectively. However, what a lot of people forget is that all of the above five senses become obsolete, and can be switched off, if one vital organ is missing: *the brain*.

A point I often make with my biology students is that we see, hear, taste, smell and touch with our brains! We don't see with our eyes, we don't hear with our ears and we certainly don't feel touch because of our skin alone. All of these sense receptors just mentioned are tasked with one job only: to send information to the brain to be processed. Once the brain processes the necessary information, we then feel the intended sensation.

Evolution has ensured that our brains are hard-wired to remember information generated by all five senses. It is essential that we can do this, otherwise we would not be able to survive. Immanuel Kant puts this very eloquently:

> *"All our knowledge begins with the senses, proceeds then to the understanding, and ends with reason. There is nothing higher than reason."*
>
> ### Immanuel Kant (Author of Critique of Pure Reason)

When students have a good rapport with their teachers and are genuinely interested in the subject being taught, they acquire the self-confidence and motivation to pursue their learning with hard-work and enthusiasm. 'Interest' is a funny human condition because we often make the mistake of thinking that it's just something that each person has an affinity for, based upon their life experiences or even the way they were born. However, the real truth is that the effective teacher behaviours outlined in these first two chapters can literally change students' lives as they go from 'liking' a subject, to wanting to be the best student in the class!

You're about to see the effect this had on the motivation of one of my former students, who is also one of the illustrators of this book: Ms Sutthiya Lertyongphati. Back in 2009 I was her IGCSE Chemistry teacher, and she became so motivated to learn this difficult subject (with the added pressure of learning it in her second language: English), that she made a resolution to herself to produce the best class notes possible. When CfBT inspectors saw these notes that same year, they said that were 'the best they had ever seen'. I've included them on the next five pages.

Date : 2 MARCH

TOPIC: MANUFACTURE OF ALUMINIUM AND CHLORIDE AND SODIUM HYDROXIDE

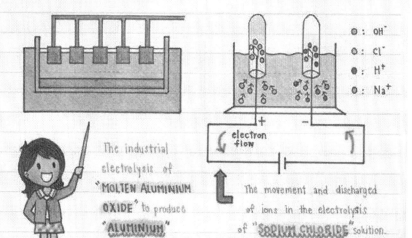

⊙ : OH⁻
○ : Cl⁻
● : H⁺
○ : Na⁺

The industrial electrolysis of "MOLTEN ALUMINIUM OXIDE" to produce "ALUMINIUM"

electron flow

The movement and discharged of ions in the electrolysis of "SODIUM CHLORIDE" solution.

Date : 3 MARCH

TOPIC : EXOTHERMIC AND ENDOTHERMIC REACTION

EXOTHERMIC : energy is **released** into the surrounding

ENDOTHERMIC : energy is **absorbed** from the surrounding

Date:

No:

Date: 16 MARCH

TOPIC: EFFECT OF LIGHT ON THE SPEED OF REACTIONS

As the light intensity increases ⬆, the speed of the reaction also increases ⬆, because light energy gives out HEAT ENERGY ⬇ ⬇ ⬇ ⬇

Date: 17 MARCH

TOPIC: USE OF SILVER SALT IN PHOTOGRAPHY AND PHOTOSYNTHESIS

In photography , Silver bromide is being used.

$$\text{LIGHT COLOR} \left\{ \begin{array}{c} AgBr \\ Ag^{2+} \end{array} \right. \xrightarrow[\text{REDUCED}]{\text{LIGHT}} Ag^+ \ (AgBr)$$

Depending on the amount of light,
A different shade of grey is produced.

 ※ PHOTOSYNTHESIS:

$$6CO_2 + 6H_2O \longrightarrow C_6H_{12}O_6 + O_2$$

(OXYGEN IS REDUCED)

$$6CO_2 + 6H_2O \longrightarrow C_6H_{12}O_6 + 6O_2$$

Date : 21 APRIL

TOPIC : STEEL- MAKING

The iron produced by the blast furnace is known as "**PIG IRON**" or "**CAST IRON**" and is **NOT PURE**. It contains 4% of carbon which makes itself *brittle*.

The carbon content is reduced by burning it off as **carbon monoxide** and **carbon dioxide**. Any sulphur contamination is oxidised to **sulphur dioxide**. This basic oxygen process is carried out in a "**TILTING FURNACE**."

① The furnace is charged with scrap steel and molten iron.

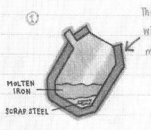

MOLTEN IRON
SCRAP STEEL

②.

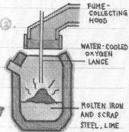

FUME - COLLECTING HOOD
WATER-COOLED OXYGEN LANCE
MOLTEN IRON AND SCRAP STEEL, LIME

O_2 is blown in through an OXYGEN LANCE.

③.

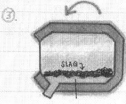

SLAG
MOLTEN STEEL

The molten steel and then the slag, are poured from the furnace by tilting it in different direction.

④.

SLAG

Date: No:

Date : 25 MARCH

TOPIC : NEUTRALITY AND RELATIVE ACIDITY AND ALKALINITY IN TERMS OF
pH MEASURED USING "UNIVERSAL INDICATOR PAPER"

✳ Rules for pH scale:
- acids have a pH "LESS THAN 7"
- the more "ACIDIC" the solution, the "LOWER" the pH

pure water
- Neutral substances, such as have a pH of 7

- Alkaline have a pH "GREATER THAN 7"
- the more "ALKALINE" the solution, the "HIGHER" the pH

-pH scale-

pH   1 2 3 4 5 6 7 8 9 10 11 12 13 14

STRONGLY ACIDIC   WEAKLY ACIDIC   NEUTRAL WEAKLY ALKALINE   STRONGLY ALKALINE

Do you know what does
pH stands for?

Sure! p stands for power
and h stands for hydrogen

morning glory

Date: No.

Date: 26 MARCH

TOPIC: CHARACTERISTIC PROPERTIES OF BASES AND REACTIONS WITH ACIDS AND
WITH AMMONIUM SALTS AND EFFECT ON LITMUS

When **BASE** reacts with **ACID**:

BASE turns litmus
paper **BLUE**

$$ ACID + BASE \longrightarrow SALT + WATER $$

Bases are **INSOLUBLE** in water.
* common alkali: potassium / aluminium hydroxide

Date: 27 MARCH

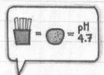

TOPIC: IMPORTANCE OF CONTROLLING ACIDITY IN SOIL

 Plant growth is affected by the acidity
of the soil.

Farmers need to know what pH suits which plants.

If the soil is too **ACIDIC**, it is usually treated by:
"**LIMING**" ⟶ neutralising the acidity of the soil.

morning glory

Active Engagement: Summary

- Make sure that your lessons begin promptly with a short starter activity. A quick starter primes the students for learning, and can be a very clever way to introduce your students to the learning outcomes and success criteria for the lesson.

- Every single lesson you teach must have clear learning outcomes, and these are most effective in focussing students' learning if the students have figured them out by themselves. Use the 'Three A's' to get your class thinking about the purpose of each lesson, before the main activities begin. You can also use the 'Three A's' to get students thinking about success criteria (the work or evidence that they will need to produce to prove that they have met the learning outcomes).

- Games should be used regularly in your lessons to make content memorable. They are also a great tool for building rapport and keeping students engaged. You can use the games in this chapter to good effect (as I have in the past) and you should start thinking about games that will work for you in your subject area. This can be achieved by modifying games that already exist (e.g. by playing hopscotch and getting the squares to represent the stages in a sequence, or by modifying 'I spy with my little eye' to include detailed clues for sophisticated concepts or content). The creative freedom you have is enormous. You may also want to create games that have never been thought of before. Also, try to include an element of class competition where possible, as this provides a huge incentive for students to work hard and encourage each other to strive for excellence.

- Make use of movement and action to stimulate as many of the five senses as you can in your lessons. It won't always be possible to target each of the five senses every lesson (or even most lessons), but you should try to at least include visual and auditory information, along with some form of movement or physical action. Don't be afraid of getting messy: students love making models out of unusual materials and doing any kind of experiment. There will be times when you try a 'multi-sensory activity' and it goes horribly wrong. Don't worry: scratch it up to experience, and your students will respect you all the more for trying.

CHAPTER 3

Behaviour Management in the High School Classroom: Learn how to keep your students interested, on-task and happy!

"You cannot control anybody else's behaviour but your own. Highly effective teachers seek to influence and manage children's behaviour. If teachers are determined to control a class they often find that classroom interactions become more hostile and they, in turn, become increasingly demanding with a heavy reliance on punishment."

Andy Vass (Co-author of The Behaviour Management Pocketbook')

Whilst working in the UK as a high school teacher from 2005 to 2008, I was exposed to a range of different whole-school and individual class 'climates'; some were hostile, some changeable and some as peaceful as a summer's day in the Lake District.

I have always found student behaviour to be a really fascinating subject. Why was it that some schools had incredibly good behaviour in the vast majority of classes, whereas others seemed to ooze confrontation, hostility, sanctions and stress? I had taught in schools in economically poor districts of North Wales where student conduct was both good and bad, and I had taught in good schools where only one or two particular classes provided problems of this type. Why was this the case? Which variables were the most vital in determining how much a student wanted to learn? Why was it that some particular teachers didn't have any problems when it came to managing student behaviour, but others were constantly using up their free time to supervise kids who they'd put on detention?

My teaching experience has taught me that there is no 'magic cure' for poor student behaviour. Every student is different, and what works for one student with one teacher may not work for a different student with a different teacher (or, incidentally, for the same student with a different teacher). The first step on the road to maximising our influence on student behaviour involves recognising that the willingness of a student to cooperate with his or her teachers involves a dynamic interplay of five key parameters:

1. **The student's home environment:** Students with a rough home life, where aspirations are low and/or rules are lax, tend to have a hard time following instructions at school. Additionally, students who are abused or neglected in some way will bring emotional baggage into school with them. This can manifest in a number of ways including attention-seeking, bullying, self-harm, emotional withdrawal, aggressiveness and depression. One important point to note here is that it's not all about the parents; there may be

many factors in a student's home environment that can negatively affect his or her desire to learn at school.

2. **Peer pressure:** 'Monkey see, monkey do' is an expression that very accurately describes the behaviour of almost every person on this planet, not just the kids we're teaching in our schools each day. As humans, we naturally gravitate towards the thought patterns of the group. In fact, Christian Crandall, a professor of social psychology at the University of Kansas, put it very succinctly when he said that "Being too much a part of a group may constrain one's ability to think outside of convention"[2]. From this perspective, we see how hard it can be for young people to escape gang mentalities and 'social norms' in their community, including drug use, alcoholism and being confrontational with people in general, not just teachers.

3. **Academic challenge:** Students who find their school work too challenging, and who get used to constant failure, soon perceive themselves as being incapable. Feeling incapable, they soon see no purpose in working hard at school. Conversely, gifted and talented students who aren't stretched enough at school soon get bored, and this leads to 'disruptive' behavioural patterns. This is particularly compounded if concepts are being repeated year after year, or if students aren't completing enough activities that suit their preferred learning styles.

4. **School ethos:** This is a major factor in determining student cooperation. Schools with overly draconian sanctions systems (e.g. where students rack up scores of documented 'warnings' and detentions on a daily basis) can see a dramatic increase in poor behaviour when these systems are implemented. Additionally, schools in which teachers do not deliver rewards and sanctions in

---

[2] Wang, S. (2011) *Under the Influence: How the Group Changes What We Think.* The Wall Street Journal. [Online] Available from: http://www.wsj.com/articles/SB1000142405274 8704436004576298962165925364 [Accessed: 17th July 2015]

a consistent manner also tend to face problems with behaviour management, as students discover what they can and can't get away with (and with whom). Additionally, my experience has taught me that schools which have a solid rewards system in place, which reinforces and encourages high performance in a range of curriculum areas (e.g. by using a 'house points' system), tend to experience better student behaviour than those which do not. This idea has been heavily reinforced by the research of leading psychologists including Dr. Lynne Rogers of the University of London, who says that "Schools where pupils' achievements are celebrated, however small, encourage pupils to be self-motivated and self-disciplined, reducing the need for staff to police their behaviour and attendance."[3]

5. *Teacher behaviours:* Let's face it, some teachers are 'good' at behaviour management and some consistently find this area of teaching to be a challenge. The rapport we build with our students, along with our professionalism across a range of areas and our reputations, are key influence factors when it comes to keeping students on task. Additionally, we must move away from the singular mindset of only being concerned about what happens in our classes, and we must adopt a group mindset where colleagues help each other, and where multiple teachers talk to students about their behaviour. This requires openness and courage, which can be quite a challenge.

In this chapter we shall explore the key ways in which effective teachers address the last item on the list: demonstrating the correct behaviours that lead to student cooperation. We'll also look at how we can make the level of academic challenge just right, and how we can contribute to a school ethos that is supportive, rewarding and pleasant for

---

[3] Rogers, L. (2008) Institute of Education, University of London. *Rewards Work Better Than Punishments Experts Say.* [Online] Available from: http://www.ioe.ac.uk/newsevents/21864.html [Accessed: 17th July 2015]

our students. A lot of what you'll read here goes hand-in-hand with the information contained in the previous chapter. Behaviour management always begins by establishing a *good rapport* with your students. Once this rapport is established, you should use the reinforcement secrets contained in this chapter to maintain a productive relationship with all of your students.

The five key parameters

Secret Number 10: Make Your Students Feel Important

I have a friend who really loves dogs. He owns a fine collection of beautiful breeds including Cavalier King Charles Spaniels, Shetland Sheepdogs and of course, everyone's favourite: Golden Retrievers. He also runs a training centre for dogs, where he and his staff teach the animals how to sit, fetch and how to let you know when they need to take a call of nature. Another section of his business involves training different breeds for various dog shows, including the world famous Crufts show in England, which is held annually. He and his team have amassed an array of medals and trophies, all finely displayed at his home, by getting his dogs to look pretty and perform various tricks and tasks. His dogs jump through hoops, climb up platforms, run through tunnels, catch tennis balls, jump over hurdles and meander speedily around obstacles to get those shiny objects of recognition that are finely displayed for all and sundry to see. Needless to say, my friend was very proud of his dogs and what he saw as *his* achievements.

As I was preparing to write this chapter, I was thinking about the dynamic that my friend represents. He was incredibly proud of all of those trophies and medals that were glistening brightly in the many display cabinets at his home. However, his dogs couldn't give a damn about those trophies and medals; all they wanted was food, water and some attention to make them happy.

This short description of my friend's passion for his business demonstrates an essential facet of the human condition, which I have found to be true for adults and children alike: we all want to feel important. This is a feature unique to humans, and it's a characteristic that distinguishes us from animals.

Every high school student you will encounter, no matter what their domestic situation is or how much peer pressure they are under, craves a sense of personal importance just like you and I do. It's the reason why we wear posh designer labels, why we brag about our new car or house on social media and why we beautify images of ourselves using various apps on our smart phones. It's also the reason why a lot of young people turn to drugs, join gangs and get involved in thug culture. The trick with students is to make sure that they are receiving their *validation*, their sense of importance, from positive sources.

For our students, the best way that we can make them feel empowered and important in a positive way is by enacting the following steps:

1. *Find out what the strengths, hobbies and interests of each of your students are:* This can be daunting, as you've probably got a whole gaggle of students that you teach and it's hard to remember everything about everyone. If you have too, buy a special notebook and write down snippets of information that you pick up. Is Thomas exhibiting his artwork at a local gallery this weekend? Write it down. Does Cassandra love fashion design and magazines like Cosmopolitan? Write it down. Did Jason score a goal at lunchtime football? Write it down.

2. *Act on the information you have gathered:* Use the information to engage your students in their lessons. If the output of a task or project is open to negotiation, then suggest a way for a particular student to produce that output in a way that is personal to them. Does Damon like boxing? Get him to create an animation or movie of a boxing match in which each boxer represents one side of the debate. They can say counter phrases whilst they box, and the winner will represent the argument that Damon agrees with the most. When doing group work, assign roles to each student based on their strengths, and make it clear why you have chosen each student for each role. I once had a student who was famous for being confrontational, and he was the figment of every teacher's worst nightmare in that school. However, I noticed quickly that he was very good at art, so I made him the class 'art director', where his job was to check each student's presentation. He loved the positive attention, and he became my most compliant and hard-working student. I also took a special interest in him by going along to the art room to look at his work, and view his pieces in a local art gallery. This extra effort on my part really paid off, and other subject teachers were amazed at the change they saw in him.

3. *Always turn a negative into a positive:* Have you just taught a student who 'played up' or had a 'tantrum'? Has one of your students just had a 'bad day'? Make a special note of this, sit down

with the student and offer your help and guidance. Focus on the positives of this situation, and what the student did well. Perhaps this time the student didn't swear – now that's a positive and a step in the right direction. Maybe your student was frustrated because they couldn't quite make their work 'perfect' – brilliant, this shows a desire to do well and try your best. Tell the student how pleased you are that they care about their work so much and offer more time to get it done if needs be. Maybe another student annoyed the kid who played up; offer a number of solutions to the student such as a seating plan and the chance to have a 'time out'. Get your 'problem students' to reflect on solutions, and praise them for being reflective and proactive in wanting to move forwards, and not backwards.

4. *Focus on the long-term goals of the student:* Some students are completely unsure of what they want to do in life even when they reach 18 years of age, when they're about to start out at university or find employment. Others take time to develop their goals as they mature through high school and still others are very sure what they want from life since their first day in Year 7. Whatever the situation may be, you must remind your students that there's a bright and happy light at the end of the tunnel (and it's not an oncoming train!). Talk regularly with your students about their goals, ambitions and strengths, and constantly make them feel like they can achieve those goals by being supportive and enthusiastic for them. When students can see that there is a real purpose to school life; that all of these 'pointless lessons' can actually make your dreams come true, they tend to work harder. However, you, as a teacher, need to constantly reinforce this and it can take some time and effort before positive progression is seen. Stay strong, have faith and I guarantee that your efforts will pay massive dividends!

5. *Use rewards more than sanctions, and make them sincere:* When a student accomplishes something, and is then rewarded for this

accomplishment, this reinforces the positive behaviour/process that lead to the outcome. However, the extent to which this reinforcement is maximized depends upon the *depth, relevance and sincerity* of the *feedback* given to the student. We're all so very busy, and it can really tempting to just sign that house point box in the student's planner, or hand out that merit sticker, with little conversation afterwards. However; if we're going to be effective behaviour managers, then we need to spend more time giving sincere and relevant feedback to our students that focuses on the effort or process that went into the work that was produced. Always sit down with your students, especially those who have a reputation for being disruptive, and talk with them about their accomplishments. Tell the student how happy you are, and give a good reason (e.g. "I was so pleased that you took the time to draw large, labeled diagrams in this work. You also asked lots of questions, and you tried your best to avoid distractions"). This is actually quite simple when we think about it: all we're trying to do is reinforce the behaviour that we want to see repeated again in the future.

Making your students feel important, or valued, is probably the most important factor in ensuring that you have a positive relationship with them (and, hence, lessons in which behaviour is good). One of the most memorable examples of this takes me back to my first teaching post in Thailand, when I was teaching Personal, Social and Health Education (PSHE) to a group of Year 8 students. At that time, I was taking the students through the Expect Respect™ programme, and we were covering themes that centred around domestic abuse and neglect. At the end of my first lesson with this group, a very shy and withdrawn young girl spoke with me privately and said that she enjoyed the lesson because it made her reflect on what was happening in her home environment. She then revealed to me something which almost shocked me to a frail state of nervousness as a young teacher – she told me she was self-harming, and she showed me the scars on her arms.

The first thing I did at that moment was talk about the positives of this situation, and I praised her for having the courage to speak to someone. I asked her what she thought of the lesson, and she said that she could empathise with the people involved in the scenarios we had discussed. I said that that was a brilliant quality to have, and that she could use this in her career when she leaves school. She left with a very bright smile on her face, and I could tell that she felt empowered. I saw her domestic situation as a positive, because it gave her the experience she needed to help other people in similar situations.

After our conversation, I referred her to our school counselor who worked with her twice a week to talk about what she was going through and how to move forward. She told her counselor how she felt so refreshed by her conversation with me, and how she felt that she could be a counselor too!

As time went by, I constantly reinforced my belief and professional interest in this student. When we covered career clusters in later PSHE lessons, she was keen to talk about how she wanted to be a person who cared for, and helped, others. She talked boldly about her plans to make people happy, and she would allude to her life experiences as being valuable in making her a strong person. Prior to this transformation, this young lady was famous for crying in class, and would often not take part in group activities. My belief in her, along with the help provided by other staff members, transformed her into a self-confident, determined person.

I am not ashamed to say that I was rather tearful when she got accepted into university to study occupational therapy five years later. She is now a professional, mature and empowered young woman who has a dream and a mission to help the people she comes across in her day-to-day life. I must admit, I can't take all of the credit for this, as many individuals in the school worked with her to empower her to be bold enough to face life's setbacks and move forward. However, I like to think that that first conversation she had with me all of those years ago was the spark that set the forest fire of her ambition raging through the wilderness of her life.

Secret Number 11: Speak up, and Look for Positive Deviants

Have you ever noticed that there are some teachers in your school who never seem to have behaviour management issues? They just seem to be able to teach their classes with no disruption whatsoever or, at the very least, they deal with disruption or poor behaviour quickly, fairly and consistently. These people are positive deviants[4]: they should have the same problems as you do, but they don't. These are people you can learn from, and who you should consult with regularly.

In many schools around the world teachers are made to feel inferior if they admit to having a problem. I have experienced this kind of culture first hand, and it can be very disempowering. You speak up and you say "I'm having problems with 'student x', he just never seems to listen", and one of your colleagues pipes in with a "Really, well he's fine for me". The person who dishes out this quick and smarmy reply is either a positive deviant, who you can learn from, or they're lying so that they can make themselves look good in public. If conversations of this type are commonplace in your school, then it can be difficult to have the courage to speak up when you have a problem. However, it is absolutely essential that you do speak up because you'll probably find someone who can help you when the problem is in its infancy, allowing you to deal with it before it becomes a lot worse.

---

[4] I am borrowing the phrase 'positive deviants' from the excellent book 'Influencer: The New Science of Leading Change' by Joseph Grenny, Kerry Patterson, Ron McMillan and Al Switzler. I strongly recommend this book to any teachers who aspire to positively influence their students or who wish to be effective school managers.

Case Studies: Schools That Have Turned Behaviour Around

St Peter's Catholic High School (Gloucester, England)

This is s secondary inner-city Catholic comprehensive school for 11 to 18 year olds, that caters for a range of abilities. There are 1,700 pupils on the school roll, and in November 2012, the school was rated by Ofsted (the UK's schools inspectorate) as 'outstanding' in behaviour.

School ethos

The school has developed a positive and supportive environment in which teachers and pupils respect each other. To help create this atmosphere, the school refers to each form group, including the teacher, as a 'family' with responsibility, respect and care for each other.

Methodologies

The school uses the Schools Information Management System (SIMS) to record and manage behaviour. The school records both good and bad behaviour, and this allows staff to monitor trends and patterns.

The school uses SIMS to place pupils on an e-report. This means that teachers monitor and report on the behaviour of each student. This report is used by the school to track progress and is automatically sent home to parents.

Where a student continues to be disruptive, the form tutor (the person responsible for that student) is able to create an individual behaviour support programme. Parents are invited to be involved with this process and together they set short-term, achievable targets for the pupil to help improve their behaviour.

Inclusion unit

When students continually behave inappropriately they are taken out of lessons and placed in the inclusion unit for a day. The inclusion unit is supervised by senior staff, with a separate timetable, and class teachers provide the pupil with their work for the day. The separate timetable means pupils are not able to socialise with their friends for the entire day and, at least in part because of this, it is an effective deterrent against poor behaviour.

Comment

One of the key features behind this school's 'outstanding' rating for behaviour stems from the fact that every student is *made to feel important*. This sense of importance is created by the form group 'family', where every student is made to feel respected and a part of something bigger than themselves. This can be particularly empowering for students who don't have positive relationships with their family members at home.

This school is realistic in its approach to behaviour management. School administrators realise that good student behaviour is not solely dependent on the actions of individual teachers in individual classes, but is instead influenced by the dynamic interplay between parents, students, school management, teachers and the physical environment of the school. Parents are encouraged to be involved in each students individual behaviour support programme, and targets are set which are achievable (and, therefore, believable!)

Behaviour is monitored rigorously at this school, with staff having access to the school-wide SIMS system. This ensures that teachers can support each other by speaking with students when they behave poorly in their colleagues' classes. Additionally, it means that negative behaviour is always followed up appropriately, and nothing is allowed to go 'under the radar'. This encourages self-responsibility within each student, whilst being non-invasive at the same time.

Source: UK DEPARTMENT FOR EDUCATION. (2014). *Managing behaviour and bullying in schools case studies.* Contains public sector information licensed under the Open Government Licence v3.0.

Key steps to take when seeking help from colleagues

1. *Speak up and admit when you have a problem*: You can speak with a line manager or even another colleague you trust. If it's a whole-class issue in which you're having problems with disruption from multiple students, then try to find other teachers who teach that same class. Ask for their advice. The same rule applies if you're having a problem with an individual student – find out who his or her other teachers are, and talk with them.

2. *Identify positive deviants*: Find all of those teachers who have a positive relationship with the student, or group of students, you're having problems with.

3. *Ask those positive deviants to observe your lessons*: This can be hard to do, because most teachers absolutely hate lesson observations. However, you must see this as a massive opportunity to learn from the positive deviant who's observing you. Besides, just by asking this person to observe your class you'll be making them feel important, and they'll probably like you all the more for it. Make sure you seek feedback from the observer, and be sure to record everything that he or she says about your lesson.

4. *Observe the positive deviants*: Book a time when you can see the positive deviant 'in action'. Try to observe them whilst they're teaching the same students, and make lots of notes (or even ask for permission to video the lesson). Try to think of all of the things that this person is doing to reinforce and promote positive behaviour, and then try to model this in your lessons. You may even ask the positive deviant to observe you again at this point, if you wish, just so that you can 'fine tune' the new techniques that you have learned.

5. *Be sure to sincerely thank the positive deviants* when they have helped, and don't forget to sing their praises to senior management and your colleagues too. For most people this seems silly – after all, why would you want to praise someone else's

teaching? I assure you: doing this will help you to build a strong professional relationship base that will really help if times get tough, or if you need help in the future. You'll also be contributing to a whole-school ethos of mutual respect and openness, which can only serve to create a positive culture for everyone. You'll also make a lot of friends in the process!

This seems so obvious, doesn't it? - Find your positive deviants and then model their behaviours. However, in most schools this never happens, and it's mostly because our pride gets in the way. We don't want to seem inferior to others by admitting we have a problem, and the rigour of school appraisal processes have turned lesson observations into an apprehensive, stressful part of a teacher's life. This is incredibly regrettable and we must overcome this closed-mindedness and fear of being judged if we are to really learn from our colleagues and become the champion teachers we can be.

Secret Number 12: You Can Learn From Your Students Too

One of my former colleagues once said "If you want to know who's a good teacher, then ask the students". I couldn't agree more with this statement. Most people, when confronted with this, will say something like 'Aha, well, kids are just gonna say that they love the teachers who don't give them homework to do". Hmmm, I don't think so. My observations after ten years of teaching in a wide variety of schools in both the UK and here in Thailand have told me that kids like the teachers who are rigorous, consistent, fair, entertaining, caring and who enact all of the behaviours needed to maintain good teacher-student rapport.

With this in mind, consider doing some kind of student led self-appraisal every so often. Perhaps you can set up an anonymous Google form for your kids to fill in, which asks crucial questions about your performance as a teacher (e.g. How quickly you hand back homework). You may wish to use some resources that are ready made for you, available online. Whatever you choose, make sure that the evaluation form is well-structured, and doesn't involve too much 'creative freedom'. I remember one teacher who simply asked her Year 11 class to write down "what was wrong" with her lessons, and many students wrote some very scathing (and unhelpful) comments. This was also rather counterproductive, as it reinforced the idea in the students' minds that their teacher was 'just no good', and was desperately trying to get things in order. Alleviate this issue by doing a student-led self evaluation regularly, making it a 'mechanical' part of your teaching (e.g. by doing one at the end of every half-term). If you can get this set up as whole-school practice, then that's even better!

Online resources: Teacher evaluation by students

The following URL's provide links to sample forms that you can use with your students when evaluating your performance as a teacher. You may wish to adapt these to suit the needs of your classes.

- *http://cft.vanderbilt.edu/guides-sub-pages/student-feedback/#inclass* University of Vanderbilt Center for Teaching. Lots of really useful forms and ideas here.

- *http://www.celt.iastate.edu/teaching-resources/document-your-teaching/student-evaluation-of-teaching/sample-questions/* Iowa State University, Center for Excellence in Teaching. Lots of good questions here, including some which focus on the student's own contributions to class.

- *http://www.rucharacter.org/file/Microsoft%20Word%20%20Teacher%20Evaluation%20by%20Students(1).pdf* 2005 Schools of Character, Award Winning Practices. This form has a very handy 1 – 5 scoring point system, and offers a quick way for students to provide lots of useful feedback to their teachers.

Case Studies: Schools That Have Turned Behaviour Around

St Benedict Academy (Derby, England)

Saint Benedict Academy is a Catholic school for 11 to 18 year-olds, which also welcomes pupils from other faiths. The school takes pupils from across the city of Derby, resulting in a diverse socioeconomic and ethnic mix. In November 2012, the school was rated by Ofsted as 'good' in behaviour.

The turnaround centre

The school has a turnaround centre that offers a modified curriculum and specialist behaviour management support to students who can't learn in mainstream school, frequently due to persistent disruptive behaviour. A student will usually spend a minimum of 6 weeks in the turnaround centre, depending on their need, with the aim of being reintegrated into mainstream school.

Pupils in the turnaround centre are monitored closely to ensure the intervention meets their specific needs. There is a daily written log, parents are contacted every week, and there are 3 and 6 week reviews to evaluate progress. When the pupil returns to the main school they are accompanied by a learning support assistant who supports their move back into regular classes.

The 'C' system

The school also has a range of measures to tackle negative conduct before it escalates into persistent poor behaviour. The school created the 'C' system to help staff consistently tackle behaviour:

C1 means 'Chance': recorded	This gives the pupil a chance to stop the behaviour and, if they do, nothing is recorded
C2 means 'Choice':	This means that the pupil chose to continue behaving badly and will receive a 30-minute detention during which the pupil and teacher will talk about the behaviour
C3 means 'Consequence':	This means that the pupil has continued to misbehave and will be removed from the classroom to the isolation room. The pupil will receive a 30-minute detention and a Friday after-school detention.

Comments

The system that this school has implemented is highly effective for four main reasons:

- **Language:** The terminology used by this system makes it very clear to students that they first have a 'chance' to make things better when they slip-up, and then after that point they are choosing to misbehave and will ultimately be carried forward in the system. This places the responsibility of good behaviour solely in the hands of each student.
- **Fairness:** Students do not receive the main consequence until they have misbehaved three times in a row. This allows each student the opportunity to make amends before things become serious. Unfortunately, in some schools that have systems like this, the main consequences come very early on, sometimes after the first 'warning'. All this serves to do is create an environment of stress and antagonism for everyone concerned, and it can actually cause behaviour to get worse.
- **Consistency:** This system is implemented by every teacher in the school, and each student is informed about the system during tutor time and upon starting their first class of the year.
- **Feedback:** At stage 2 (Choice), the student sits with the teacher and talks about the behaviour. Again, this is a practice that is overlooked by far too many schools. When students are given the opportunity to articulate the process that led to the poor behaviour, they are better able to understand and spot the 'triggers' that set them off on this course of action. Additionally, the teacher has an opportunity to present his or her point of view, and with most students this leads to a mutual agreement and a 'fresh start' when the next lesson begins.

Source: UK DEPARTMENT FOR EDUCATION. (2014). *Managing behaviour and bullying in schools case studies.* Contains public sector information licensed under the Open Government Licence v3.0.

You may also find this newsletter from Stanford University very useful when designing your own student-led teaching evaluation:

- *web.stanford.edu/dept/CTL/Newsletter/student_evaluations.pdf*

The benefits that come from students evaluating their teachers in an anonymous, guided way are obvious: the teacher receives honest feedback directly from the target audience. If this is supported by a nurturing and open-minded school-ethos, and if the teacher acts upon this feedback, then it can lead to dramatic improvements in student engagement as well as offering a powerful tool for professional growth.

Secret Number 13: Focus on the Outcome, not the Negative Behaviour

When I first started out as a Newly Qualified Teacher, I found that managing student behaviour was quite a challenge. If a student wasn't focussed on his work I would say something like "Luke, why aren't you concentrating" or "David, I'm getting fed up with your lack of focus". If a student was talking when they shouldn't I would blurt out an "I've told you once already not to talk, and yet you still continue". Any experienced teacher will straight away spot that these kinds of teacher responses are absolutely foolish, and only serve to encourage confrontation. Why? It's simple when I analyse it now, many years later – I was focussing on the negative personality trait of each student, and not on the work that I had set for them to do.

Nowadays, whenever I spot similar behaviour (a student who's not on-task), I will intervene with a "Hey Jack, how's that work going?" or a "Let's take a look at this work, John". I will then walk up to the student and actually look at the work being done, and I'll pick out some good points. "Now that's great, Sarah. I love how you've coloured in that Bunsen Burner so well. I know that this is going to be a brilliant piece of work when it's finished. I really need it to be done in the next fifteen minutes though. Do you think that would work for you?" If the disruption or distraction continues I'll pipe in with a "Come on Sarah, I know you can do this".

The result of my altered approach to low-level disruption: I create a much more positive environment in my classroom than if I am constantly referring to negative behaviour, and my students feel valued and empowered to do their best. Of course, there will always be some students who still won't respond positively to this, and you'll then need to use whichever sanctions system your school has in place. However, for the vast majority of students this approach works as an encouraging, positive and friendly way to keep them on-task.

Secret Number 14: Learn to Like Your Students

I'll never forget one classic experience in my role as a young, enthusiastic teacher of science back in England. I had been given responsibility for a Year 9 class (age 13 – 14 years old), and I was to be their science teacher for every science lesson each week. This class had a number of disruptive 'characters' in it: students who had become infamous for their bad behaviour. However, I had never met these students before (this was my first year of teaching at this school) and it was a fresh start for them.

My lessons started out brilliantly. I got to know each and every student; I took an interest in them as young people and I rewarded them consistently using the school's merit system. I tried my best to include as many practical activities and games as possible (in my attempt to address the needs of every learning style in the class), and the classroom environment was extremely positive. Many of my colleagues were having problems with these students, but I was having a great time teaching them.

Then, everything started to change. Construction work began on the school in an area that was adjacent to the classroom I was teaching these kids in. It became so noisy that I often couldn't hear the students speak.

The noise also added to a general mood of low focus and distraction and, I'm ashamed to say, I even found myself shouting "shut up" to some of the students at one point. The negativity built up to the point that my enjoyment of teaching this class waned, and I secretly started to dislike some of these students. The kids sensed it, and they started to dislike me too.

Eventually, my head of department realised how bad the noise was and my class were transferred to another science lab. However, by that point negative behaviour patterns had started to become habitual, and it took time for me to re-establish the pleasant learning environment that we had enjoyed at the start of the academic year. Upon analysis, with the benefit of that wonderful evaluator of life: hindsight; it can be tempting to think that the noise was the cause of the problems faced in this situation. However, it was actually the negative environment that I had created through my change in behaviour which really initiated the disruptiveness that followed.

Your students are human, just like me and you, and they're not stupid: they can sense when a teacher (or other individual) doesn't like them. As humans, we have a natural affinity towards those people who we like, and who like us, and your students will certainly be more compliant and happy if they know that you genuinely care about them and their learning. No matter how infamous a student or class may be, no matter what the student wrongdoings of the past are, we must learn to spot the positive attributes of our kids and learn to like them as individuals. Once we have a sincere sense of compassion for our students, it is much easier to implement the rapport-building and behaviour management techniques outlined in this book.

We must learn to spot the positive attributes of our kids and learn to like them as individuals.

Secret number 15: Be Fair and Consistent

If your school has a distinct sanctions system in place, then it's essential that it is applied consistently (otherwise it won't work). By consistent, I mean the following:

- It is used by every teacher in the same way. This can be achieved by training staff in the methodologies behind the system, along with constant reinforcement by senior managers. If one teacher applies the sanctions system in a looser, more relaxed way than another teacher does, then this is naturally going to cause problems.

Case Studies: Schools That Have Turned Behaviour Around

Blessed Trinity Roman Catholic School (Burnley, England)

The school is for 11 to 16 year olds. Students come from both privileged and deprived backgrounds. In 2011 the school was rated as 'inadequate' in behaviour by Ofsted (the UK schools inspectorate), but in 2013 the school was rated as 'good' for behaviour.

Head's breakfast

The headteacher introduced the head's breakfast on his arrival at the school. Once a week the headteacher meets with a targeted group of 8 to 12 pupils from a particular cohort, for example those who have free school meals, special educational needs or who are in top set classes.

Pupils are offered a sandwich and the headteacher asks them:
- What is your favourite lesson?
- What would you change about this school if you could?
- Does bullying happen in this school?

Initially these sessions were an opportunity for the head to get to know the pupils and vice versa. Now they are a useful forum for pupils to raise issues, feel they are listened to and for staff to hear about the school from a pupil's point of view.

Listening to staff

Soon after the 'inadequate' Ofsted rating, the school set up the 'Staff Strategy Group' which included a local authority advisor, senior staff, governors, teachers, and non-teaching staff. This group gave classroom teachers and support staff the opportunity to:
- Share their actual experiences of behaviour in the classroom and around the school building
- Enable senior staff to share their vision for the school

Together, they wrote the behaviour stages system and set out the expectations of pupils both in and out of class.

Since making an improvement in the school, the strategy group no longer exists but there are other opportunities for staff to have a say. The school started an annual staff survey, which is followed up with an 'open staff meeting' to discuss issues that emerged in the survey results. In 2011, the survey found that only 38% of staff felt that behaviour was well managed, compared to 90% a year later (a dramatic improvement).

'Ladder' of detentions

Senior staff are visible to both pupils and classroom teachers in managing behaviour. They implemented a 'ladder' of detentions for pupils who do not turn up for their detentions. At each step, the detention is escalated to a more senior member of staff.

- The first detention is with the class teacher who is disciplining the pupil for poor behaviour in their lesson
- If the pupil does not attend, they are given a detention with the curriculum leader for that particular subject
- If this detention is not attended, they are given a detention with a senior member of staff

Comment

Once again, we see how showing a genuine interest in students, along with listening to their points of view, empowers them with a sense of importance. This sense of importance allows the students at this school to contribute honestly to constructive dialogue centred on the school environment, and the school administrators are consistent in acting upon it.

One interesting point about this school is that teachers were allowed the chance to share their voice, so that the real-life practicalities of school-wide behaviour management could be understood and analysed. The open staff meetings allow teachers to continue to have their say, making them feel important and empowered. Feeling empowered and supported, they are able to work with students and colleagues to manage behaviour positively. The 'ladder of detentions' is also a clever way to make behaviour management a collective responsibility.

The approach taken by this school has clearly worked. To go from an 'inadequate' rating for behaviour to a 'good', in the space of only two years, is quite an achievement.

Source: UK DEPARTMENT FOR EDUCATION. (2014). *Managing behaviour and bullying in schools case studies.* Contains public sector information licensed under the Open Government Licence v3.0.

- Within each class you must apply the sanctions system fairly to each student. There can be no favouritism in teaching, and you must treat each student equally (unless there are extenuating circumstances which have understandably affected the behaviour of the student).

If your school does not have a distinct sanctions or 'warning' system in place, then you need to devise one of your own. My advice on this would be:

1. Try not to be too strict. Give students a chance to redeem themselves in the first instance.

2. Always talk to the student about the poor behaviour that has caused them to be sanctioned. Discuss the process that lead to this situation unfolding, and discuss ways to improve upon this in future.

3. Document everything! Keep records of when instances of poor behaviour occur, and what you did to sanction the student. You may need to refer to this documentation later on when speaking with a parent or a senior manager.

Secret Number 16: Get Your Students to Devise Their Own Set of Rules, Responsibilities and Consequences

It's often a good idea to sit with your class at the start of the academic year, and have a 'class meeting' with them. I personally like to split my class into small groups and get them to write down answers to the following connectives:

- As a student in this class I should always ....

- I enjoy learning from teachers who ....

- If I do not follow my class rules, then my teacher should ....

At the end of this activity, I like to mix up the groups and get different students to edit the lists. After this, we get together and devise a whole class set of rules, responsibilities and sanctions.

This can be a particularly rewarding activity, especially with younger students (it's probably not as important to do this with a group of advanced learners, but it can be effective with individual students who, for whatever reason, do not have the correct learning attitude), since the students come up with the rules themselves. Having come up with these rules themselves, they become empowered to follow them because it's personal to them and it seems reasonable (since the students are the ones who processed information in the task to generate the outcome). Be careful though, especially in schools where there is a 'global' rewards and sanctions system in place, as you'll be expected to follow this school-wide system religiously. However, even in this case, it is still good for students to go through the process of reflecting upon reasonable behaviours, responsibilities and consequences. It can also be a good opportunity for you to remind them about how the school's sanction system works.

Secret Number 17: You Don't Have to Punish Everything

Michael was a student who was famous for being confrontational. If he felt he was being unfairly treated, or even being 'told what to do', he would waste no time in arguing his point. He was constantly on detention, and school had become quite a negative environment for him.

On one particular Tuesday morning, Michael had had quite a rough time. His mum had been away from home for two days, and he had his mates stay over at his house. It later emerged that they had drank alcohol together and had partied quite hard. After missing school for one day, Michael decided that he wasn't going to miss school today (he was afraid of the school calling his mum about it). On this particular morning he had skipped breakfast after waking up late, had missed the school bus and had to walk to school.

He arrived at my science class visibly exhausted, and just walked in without even a knock on the door. He then proceeded to take out a can of cola and started drinking it. This is an absolute no-no in a science lab – no eating or drinking whatsoever, and our departmental policy was to issue a detention on the spot. "Michael, it's good to see you, but you know that you can't drink in here. That's an automatic detention".

Well, that was the fuse that really set him off! "Are you (insert expletive here) kidding me! I've only just come into school and I'm on one detention already! For (insert second expletive here) sake!". Now, most new teachers (and some experienced ones too) would probably respond to this in a gut, emotional way, by enacting whichever sanction they felt was necessary. Not only had Michael broken a class rule by drinking in the lab, but he'd also answered back to a teacher and had used swear words! Surely he needed to be hung, drawn and quartered, right?

I knew better. I knew that raising the level of confrontation would only serve to make matters worse, and would help absolutely no one – not him, not my other students, not me, not anyone. I calmly gave my class a task to do, and I walked over to Michael to have a chat with him.

"Okay, Michael, now how do you think I should respond to what you just did?"

"I dunno sir, but I swear down I ain't done nothing wrong and I'm now on detention"

"Okay, I'm willing to listen to you Michael. I respect you as a person, but I think we both know that you did do something a little bit wrong this morning. Do you agree?"

"Okay, yeah I swore and I had a drink. I haven't had a drink since I woke up, I'm thirsty. I can't learn if I'm thirsty"

"Okay, Michael, I'll tell you what. I'm supposed to automatically give you a detention for your actions this morning, but I'm going be fair with you. I realise that you've probably had a rough morning today, so I'm willing to do a deal with you. How about I give you a few minutes to finish your drink outside, and then I'd like you to come inside and produce your best work for me. I know that you can do this Michael, because you've produced some brilliant work for me in the past. If you can give me a good piece of work by the end of the lesson, then I'll probably forget about the detention."

"Okay. That sounds fair"

"Thank you, Michael. I really appreciate your understanding"

What was the result of this? Michael did indeed try his best to complete the work, and he was let off with the detention. If Michael had decided not to do what we had agreed, then he would have been given that detention (and he knew that).

We have to remember that some students just can't help getting themselves 'stuck in a rut' sometimes. Whilst I don't endorse relaxing sanctions all of the time (that would only make behaviour worse, as students would soon learn that they can get away with being non-compliant), it is sometimes necessary to turn a blind eye. In this example, Michael was given a fresh start and he ended up having quite a productive day. Had I have formally gone through our school's sanctions system in this case, then the confrontation would have escalated, Michael would have found himself in all sorts of trouble, and he would probably have missed some of his classes for that day because he would have been placed in the isolation room. As a teacher, you need to gauge when it is appropriate to relax the rules a little bit, and this only comes with experience.

Secret Number 18: Use Body Language

Where possible, it is always best to stop low-level disruptive behaviour in its infancy, before it manifests itself into something bigger. One of the best ways to do this is to use subtle, low-key expressions using your physiology. Some examples include:

- The 'look': When I hear low-level chatter or disruption, I often pause mid-sentence (or I pause the video or slideshow if that's the media I'm using at the time), and I simply look at the student in a way that says "We're all waiting for you to be quiet". This immediately draws the attention of all of the students, and it can have quite a large impact. I often accompany 'the look' with a half-grin, so as to not appear too aggressive or antagonistic. I also accompany this by opening my arms as if to say "Come on, you know that's wrong".

- Maintaining proximity: Being in close proximity to the disruptive student can be a very effective, non-invasive way to keep him or her on-task. I may also tap on the student's desk and point to their work, to remind them that they need to stay focussed.

- Stimulus actions: These are particularly helpful when there is a lot of whole class disruption, but you may need to give the kids a little bit of training beforehand. In the past I have used the following:

  o Clapping twice, after which the students all clap three times (this is a ritual they have memorised)

  o Singing "If you're happy and you know it clap your hands" and all the students clap

  o Raising my hand, after which all of the students copy by raising their hands

These low-key, non-intrusive behaviour management techniques are highly effective at stopping poor behaviour before it manifests into a confrontation. This works particularly well if it's done in a light-hearted, happy way.

Summary: Behaviour Management in the High School Classroom

- There are a number of factors that contribute to poor student behaviour. As teachers, we need to understand the dynamic that exists between each student's home environment, peer groups, the academic challenge present in each lesson and the interplay between effective teacher behaviours and a whole-school ethos. Good behaviour managers identify the factors which are causing the manifestation of the poor behaviour in the student, and then target those appropriately.

- Make your students feel important by taking a genuine interest in them. Give them special responsibilities that capitalise on their strengths, goals and hobbies and always reward their efforts sincerely.

- Speak up and seek help from your colleagues when you're having problems with behaviour management. Don't let your pride get in the way – you'll be seen as all the more professional by asking for help, rather than pretending that everything is okay.

- Consider getting your students to evaluate your performance as a teacher. Make sure that this involves a structured output; make it anonymous and, crucially, act on the advice that's been given.

- Focus on the work, not on the student's personality or negative behaviour. Keep disruptive students on-task by reminding them about the urgency of their work. Offer encouragement by stating any positives that the student has already displayed.

- Learn to like your students, even the disruptive ones. We all gravitate and work better with people we like, and your students are no different.

- Be fair and consistent. Apply rewards and sanctions fairly and equally within each class, and make sure your colleagues are doing the same!

- Get your students to come up with their own rules, expectations and reasonable consequences at the start of the academic year, and then keep reminding them of these. They've created it themselves, so it's personal to them.

- Know when to turn a blind eye, or when to recall a sanction. This takes experience and an ability to gauge the appropriateness of this for each situation.

- Use body language and your entire physiology to target poor behaviour before it manifests into something more serious. Make use of 'the look', proximity actions and physical stimuli.

CHAPTER 4

Teaching Advanced Learners: Preparing Students for Internal and External Exams

> *"Advanced learners have already developed their own successful approach to learning but we, as instructors, will not know what that is. We must provide several paths to the same content and let learners make an informed decision on which path to take."*
>
> **Dr Karen Hughes Miller (Author at Faculty Focus online magazine)**

Teachers who are preparing students for examinations always have a difficult task in hand. Some challenges that exam-preparation classes pose to course instructors are as follows:

- A very large syllabus usually has to be covered in a short space of time

- Both the subject content and the skills needed to pass the exam (commonly referred to as 'exam technique') must be taught to the students

- Revision of exam-style questions often has to be done within a limited time-frame, and is commonly left until a very late stage in the course

- The use of key vocabulary poses a considerable challenge in a number of subject areas and this challenge is further compounded if the student is not a native English speaker

- Expectations of success are usually very high, and the teacher may feel under pressure to 'perform well' from senior management, parents and, in some cases, the students themselves

- Students at this level are not always the best-behaved or studious, although the vast majority tend to have a mature approach to their learning

- Sometimes, especially at university level, the students can be so bright that they scare you! It's not uncommon for advanced learners to know more about a particular topic than the teacher!

In this chapter, we shall examine the secrets that'll help you to prepare your students thoroughly for exams, whilst at the same time making the learning process fun and meaningful. As we progress, we shall systematically tackle the key challenge areas outlined in the list above.

Secret number 19: Know the course requirements, and make sure your students know them too!

All too often, when teachers are rushed and deadlines amass, it can be easy to overlook essential syllabus content. It is absolutely vital that:

1. The students know exactly what is on the syllabus or programme of study for their course

2. The teacher plans ahead and uses the exam syllabus to guide teaching and learning

Although this may seem obvious, it is often overlooked by many teachers (especially when beginning a new job or relocating to a new area).

Bethan, a young teacher with high aspirations, had just started her new job at an IB World School. It was a prestigious position, and expectations were high. She had taught 'A' – Level Geography in her previous school, but had not taught the IB Diploma before. When she started teaching her new Year 12 class, she already had a high workload and issues to deal with at home due to relocating to her new school. To save time, she taught subject content on the 'A' – level syllabus, assuming that it equated to what was in the IB Course Guide. Since she already had the necessary resources from her previous school, she could prepare lesson materials quickly and easily.

Was this a good move on her part? By using the resources from her old school was she really preparing her students for their IB exams? The answer to both of these questions, unfortunately, is no. She was teaching content that possessed some overlap with the IB course, but it was patchy. In parts her material was either not specified in the IB Course Guide, or was too complex. After several lessons of finding the subject too difficult, a student decided to find the IB Course Guide online. When he couldn't find the material he had been taught by Bethan in there, he informed his parents, and shortly afterwards they sent an e-mail to the Head of School: Mr Brian.

Make sure that your students understand the requirements of the course, and make sure you plan ahead!

Mr Brian, being a principal with some experience of dealing with this sort of issue before, wanted to verify the facts. He arranged a meeting with Bethan, and asked her to go through her semester plan for that class. When she couldn't produce one, and when she couldn't answer the questions pertaining to the IB curriculum she was supposed to be teaching, Mr Brian was not the least bit happy. As a result of this, Bethan was made to produce detailed long-term plans for all of her classes; she was asked to e-mail the concerned parent with an explanation and she was placed under a lesson observation schedule so that her line manager could monitor her teaching. Additionally, this had the knock-on effect of reducing the students' confidence in her as their teacher. Sounds excessive? The principal didn't think so, especially when one considers that the parents at this school were all fee-paying, and rightly expected a good quality of teaching. All of this pressure, extra-workload and embarrassment could have been avoided had Bethan had simply read through the syllabus for her course and planned accordingly.

You would be surprised at how different some syllabuses can be, even when they pertain to the same examination. An Edexcel IGCSE Mathematics syllabus, for example, is significantly different to the CIE IGCSE Mathematics syllabus. Make sure that you know which syllabus you are teaching, and don't assume that it is the same as what you've taught before. Also, watch out for syllabus updates – new syllabuses can be very different to their predecessors.

Make it student-friendly

It is often a good idea to make your own 'kid-friendly' version of the course syllabus you are teaching, since this can really help both EAL and younger students to grasp the expectations of the subject being taught. Additionally, with current interest in 'smart' classrooms and VLE's shown by schools worldwide rising sharply, allowing exposure to course specifications using ICT is now more of a priority than ever before.

Innovative ways to share exam syllabus/specification outcomes:

- Make it a rule to display them in all presentations used in class (e.g. PowerPoints, Prezis and animations). Presentations can be generated by the students themselves for extra cognitive benefit.

- Use them as your lesson objectives. Use creative techniques to make the students aware of the objectives, or make the students formulate them themselves (more on this in chapter 2).

- Create revision websites which are split into the sections defined by the syllabus. Again, the students can create their own websites or they can edit yours (many VLE's allow for this).

- Make a point of emphasising key vocabulary during a lesson, and get students to use the key words learnt to figure out what the objectives were at the *end* or *middle* of a lesson. Vocabulary games such as 'splat' and 'mystery word' can help with this.

- Go through lots of exam-style questions at appropriate times in the course, and allow the students to match these questions with the outcomes of their syllabus.

- Use marketplace activities to lead groups into formulating the lesson objectives, and make sure their conclusions are linked to the syllabus outcomes

---

Secret number 20: Every lesson counts

This secret applies to classes taught at all levels of education; right from kindergarten to post-doctoral lectures. However, this secret requires special emphasis in the context of the exam-preparation class.

In almost every case, whether you're preparing students for IGCSE's, IB exams, AP, SATs, 'A' – Levels or any other external exam, you're usually in a situation where you have a very large syllabus to teach in a short amount of time. It is therefore vital that every lesson counts, and that enough material is covered per lesson to allow for a revision period before the terminal examinations begin. It is vital that you produce long-term plans that account for school holidays, field trips, special events and any other activities that will cause the students to miss your lessons in the future. The graphic on the next page goes through the main ways in which we can maximize the productivity of each advanced-level lesson that we teach.

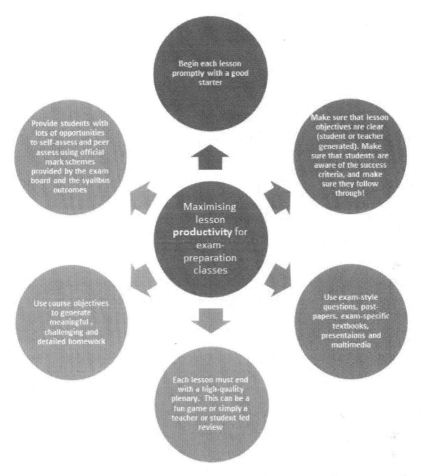

Ways in which we can maximise the productivity of each advanced lesson we teach

Maximise the effect of each lesson, and your students (and parents) will love you! If they don't thank you during the course, they'll definitely appreciate your hard work when they've completed their exams!

Secret number 20: Even advanced learners can behave like children

Think back to when you were in high school. Many people have good memories of their friends and classes, and many people can look back with pride at how hard they worked to overcome setbacks and pass their exams. Other people (myself included!) also cringe at the thought of how they were when they tried to impress the new girl, or how they tried to fit in with the crowd by copying other people or following the latest trends. At age 14 – 18 yrs old we're going through one of the most transformative times in our lives. Adolescence kicks in, along with all the hormone-fuelled drama that goes with it!

What me and you must remember, above all else, is that whilst it can be good to have a relaxed relationship with our older students, we must also not let-up on our professionalism and vigilance. This holds true particularly for teachers new to the profession.

Steven was a creative and energetic teacher who had been given an IGCSE final year mathematics class to look after. He was excited about the opportunity to teach mathematics at this high level and, being young himself, he felt that he could 'relate' well with his students. Steven quickly put all of his energy into practice and made his lessons varied, entertaining and fun. His students loved his teaching style, and were soon singing his praises to anyone who would listen. They looked forward to attending his classes, and thought that he was 'way cooler' then their previous teacher. Not wanting to lose his popularity, Steven made his lessons easy and 'cool', and made sure that homework was light. He did not reprimand students for handing in work late, and the environment he created in the classroom was so relaxed that students felt free to 'chill', listen to music and chat.

Was this a good strategy? Not really. Whilst Steven did the right thing by making his lessons fun, varied and engaging, he overlooked the two vital rules of teaching exam-preparation classes: every minute counts, and a teacher must be vigilant in ensuring that students are working hard (at the level of complexity that they are expected to work) and are on-task. Many students in Steven's class started expecting to be let off with late or substandard homework, and results on end-of-unit tests declined as time went on. When Steven finally realised what he was doing wrong (after a long and unpleasant talk with his head of department), he had a very delicate situation to deal with. He now had to clamp-down hard on his students, setting large and meaningful homework and making his lessons more complex and content-based. However, the problem was that he had *conditioned* his students into expecting the relaxed, 'fun Mr Steven', and many were resistant to the new changes. Some students even woke up the fact that they had not been taught as effectively as they should have been, and after talking with their parents, the complaints came rolling-in to the principal's inbox.

Thankfully, Steven turned this situation around and started taking the advice of his superiors. However, the whole situation was unpleasant and some of his students resented his actions till the very end, occasionally using Mr Steven's 'poor teaching' as an excuse to not revise and perform poorly on unit tests. Surely this is every advanced-level teacher's worst nightmare, right? But it could have been so easily avoided. Steven's experience teaches us the importance of maintaining our professionalism when teaching advanced-level classes.

In the course of writing this book, a former history teacher colleague of mine relayed to me the story of two of his 'A' – Level students. Setting his students some work to do, he went to the reprographics room to get some printing done, and left the two (16 and 17yr old) boys in the classroom alone. Upon his return, he found the two boys playing a card game with one another. When he asked "Have you done the questions", he was reciprocated with an "Oh, you wanted us to do them?". Needless to say, he went ballistic!

Let's not forget that it takes quite some time for children to mature into adults, especially if they've been brought up with excessive exposure to video games, smart phones, tablets, TV and junk food. 16 – 18yr old kids are exactly that: kids, and without a vigilant, consistent and professional approach an advanced-level teacher can create (or at least, ignore) problems that will impede the learning of the students.

Secret number 21: You don't have to know everything!

After teaching scores of A-level, IB, IGCSE, SAT and GMAT students over the years, often switching between several subjects in any one day, I have learnt one golden nugget of truth that I wished I had realised ten years ago: that filling your head with lots of knowledge does not guarantee that you'll teach a good lesson.

Do's and don'ts for exam-level classroom management

Do	Don't
• Make lessons varied, fun and engage the whole brain • Reprimand poor behaviour and sub-standard work. Provide sanctions that solve the initial issue (e.g. a lunchtime detention to allow the student to complete the missed homework). • Use humour to build rapport and reinforce key concepts (more on this in chapter 2). Remember to keep humour tasteful and age-appropriate.	• Make lessons so 'fun' and relaxed that students are allowed to slack-off • Create an environment where low-level disruption, poor attitudes and submission of sub-standard work is encouraged or allowed to happen • Use humour to encourage relaxation, or to divert from the content of the lesson

Let's admit it once and for all. As teachers, we don't always have all the answers and we don't know everything there is to possibly know about the subjects we're teaching. At university, even if we've reached the epic heights of gaining a PhD, we still don't learn all there is to learn about our subject areas. Advanced learners typically follow syllabuses that are complex and modern, reflecting current advances in knowledge and understanding. This can be daunting for the advanced-level teacher, especially if he has been out of the university system for a while or has not kept up to date with current advances in his subject. Thankfully, as teachers, we are not expected to know all of the details behind every topic on the syllabus. However, *we are expected to make sure that the students do!*

Any type of advanced-level setting should include a large amount of independent study and research by the students themselves. This is an essential skill that the students will need at university level and, increasingly, in upper secondary school. As teachers, we should offer as many varied opportunities as we can for our advanced learners to discover information by themselves. Besides, we all remember things better if we've figured things out independently, rather than being 'spoon-fed' the information.

Another point to note is that *whilst you don't need to know everything, you can't know nothing*. Make sure that you have read ahead in the student textbook before the lesson begins, and make sure that you at least understand the basic gist of the topic so that you have some good *primers* or *prompts* which will allow the students to explore the information further. If you've sourced PowerPoints or presentations from the internet, then make sure you've read through them and that you've edited them accordingly. It can be very tempting to quickly find a good presentation online a few minutes before a lesson begins, especially if you're in a rush. However, do be aware that sourced material online may contain excessive or limited detail, inaccuracies and inappropriate content.

Top tips for building independent learning skills (applicable to students at all levels):

- Use online simulations along with linked ICT resources to allow the students to find out about a topic themselves. There are literally hundreds of thousands of free simulations and activities online, which are often tailor-made to be fun and 'kid-friendly'. You could post links to these on your school's VLE or website, and get the students to use their laptops, tablets or smart phones to complete the activity. You could also book the school's ICT lab for a lesson, or set the task as homework if school facilities are limited. Remember to always follow up with some kind of discussion – perhaps get each student to write down five bullet points that they have learned from the simulation or activity, and then get every student to share their knowledge at the end.

- Use 'market place' activities to break down large amounts of information into bitesize chunks. The basic idea is that you provide the class with all of the information they need about a topic (e.g. all of the stages of cell division), and then you split the class into small groups, with each group focusing on only one part (e.g. one or two stages of cell division). After this you mix the groups up, and get the different 'specialists' to teach other about what they have just learned. This can be concluded with each group giving a presentation, writing a group blog post or even with each group creating a poster or website that summarises what they've just learnt.

- Provide opportunities for students to undertake group or individual projects on a regular basis. If you know that you're going to be teaching the history of the cold war next week, and it's a topic that you're not confident with, then you could get your students to complete a project all about it. Give each student or group a different theme or aspect to look into, and get them to summarise what they've learned in some way. Make sure that different groups share their information with the whole class, and use this as a focal point for a good quality topic plenary.

- Do a treasure hunt! Yes, I mean it! This is one of my favourite activities for advanced learners, but it can even be used with students as young as middle-primary school level. These are covered in more detail in chapter 5, but the basic idea is that you hide clues and information around your school for the students to hunt and find (make sure that the clues are located in classrooms that are unoccupied that lesson, and let your colleagues know that you'll be doing this activity). One method I like to use is to create QR codes that encrypt a clue (e.g. 'Go to the room where we have assembly on a Friday') and then get students to scan the QR codes using their smart phones or the school's tablets (make sure the appropriate QR reader app is installed first). When the students have picked up all of the pieces of information from each part of the school, they come back to class and put all of the pieces together to make a poster or produce a presentation using some form of virtual media (e.g. by creating an animation or cartoon using online programmes). You can make your own QR codes at www.qrstuff.com

- Get students to test out their ideas and learn through experimentation. This doesn't just apply to the sciences – it works in any subject! Provide logic diagrams or flow charts that allow students to make mistakes, and see if they can come up with conclusions by themselves. Allow students to test their ideas. Does dividing by a denominator lower than 10 always give a final answer that's smaller than the original numerator? – Get the students to test this. What's better – building a tower out of triangles or squares? – get the students to build and test! Which techniques were used to portray the sadness of the Phantom of the Opera? – Get the students to act it out and discover this by themselves. Why was Hitler such a convincing dictator? – Get the students to plan a 'convincing' task, where they have to convince a group of people about something. Get the students to reflect on which techniques they used. How does this tie-in with the techniques used by Hitler?

Secret number 22: Predicted grades are not as innocent as they seem

In my experience, predicted grades are all-too-often a headache for both the teachers who have to submit them, and for the school as a whole. Get them just right, and you'll be praised by your managers, and you'll probably make the students and parents happy too. Predict too high, and you may have to have a discussion with your line manager, in which your assessment methods for that course may be called into question. Predict too low, and that could be a good thing or a bad thing, depending on the mindset of senior management, and the school culture as a whole. Predicting too low can also result in the student not getting a provisional place at university, adding an additional responsibility on our shoulders to get it 'just right'.

If you are asked to submit predicted grades for a student, the very first thing you must do is sit down and have a talk with your line manager or the person who deals with this at a senior level. You need to find out for sure what your school means by a 'predicted grade'. Do they want a conservative 'worst-case' scenario for each student? Do they want you to predict generously, to ensure that certain students secure that university place? Does your school just want an honest prediction based on your assessment and judgment, with no serious consequences if you get it wrong? These are very important questions which, unfortunately, can have serious repercussions for your career as a teacher if you do not know the answers to them.

Unfortunately, schools are put in a pretty awkward position when it comes to predicted grades. If a school gains a reputation for providing 'inflated' or 'generous' grades to a university, then that university may blacklist the school and this can affect the successful application of any future students that apply to that university. On the other hand, many universities (especially elite institutions) may point-blank refuse to even provide a conditional offer to a student who has predicted grades that are even slightly below their requirements. This often causes tremendous concern for parents and students, and this can materialize itself as extra pressure being put on teachers to ensure that their students get offered a place a university.

You need to be absolutely crystal clear about what your school expects of you when you make a 'predicted grade'.

You need to be absolutely crystal clear about what your school's interpretation is of a 'predicted grade'. Do not be afraid to ask what the repercussions would be if you predict too high or too low – you need to know this information. The approach that has worked best for me has been to use rigorous, exam-style assessment throughout the duration of the student's course, mark harshly, and use the grades from these assessments to make a 'realistically optimistic' prediction of how the student will perform in the real exam. Some teachers I have worked with have also raised the boundaries for each assigned grade (e.g. if the actual requirement for a grade A is 75 – 80 %, then you might want to make your personal thresholds slightly higher so that you know that you are marking harshly).

It takes time and experience to become good at making accurate predictions of a student's success. Many teachers find that by becoming examiner's themselves, their knowledge of assessment standards and the course in general absolutely skyrockets, and this leads to more accurate predicted grade submissions. By knowing your course well, assessing realistically (and rigorously) and clarifying the school's stance on predicted grades, you'll be well on your way to curing this classic, chronic educational headache. So, when assigning predicted grades, remember to:

- Find out exactly what your school wants when assigning predicted grades

- Use exam-style assessments regularly and record all of your data (you may need this as evidence later on, especially if you get your predicted grades wrong)

- Consider raising the grade thresholds slightly so that you are forced to mark harshly

- If your school runs mock examinations, then make sure that yours is a past-exam paper (or similar) that the students have *never seen before*.

Secret number 23: Training is just as important as teaching

One of the first things I learnt as an 'A' – Level Chemistry teacher was that there are two sides to the advanced learning coin: what the students need to know (subject knowledge) and what the examiner wants to see (exam technique). Subject knowledge is delivered through effective *teaching*, but exam technique is built up gradually by effective *training*.

Dominique was a middle-aged French teacher who had taught first language French for twelve years at a school in Belgium. He had just relocated to Malaysia to begin work as an IGCSE and IB Diploma teacher, in a prestigious international school. His subject knowledge was high, and the role was a new challenge for him.

One of the first things that Dominique did was to gauge the students' initial knowledge of French by giving them all oral and written tests that he had used in Belgium. This gave him a good idea of which teaching strategies to use for different students, and he quickly started using activities that he knew had worked for his first language learners in the past. He used vocabulary games, listening tasks, group presentations, textbook activities and a whole array of different strategies to engage his students and maximize learning. His students generally enjoyed his lively approach to teaching, and they felt lucky to have a native French teacher to help them with their studies.

January soon came round, and his final year IGCSE and IB students were due to take their mock examinations. All teachers were instructed to use past-examination papers for the mock exam, and unfortunately for Dominique, this was the first time that he had thought to even look at the types of questions that the examiner's would ask of his students. When Dominique found a suitable past-paper for his mock examination he was mortified – the lexical density and skills required by the exam questions were way beyond his student's capabilities, and he knew it! Sure enough, when those students took the mock examination, only a small percentage achieved a respectable grade.

What had Dominique done wrong? It was simple – he'd taught his students well, but he hadn't exposed them to exam-style questions which would train them to meet the rigours of the mock examination. To add insult to injury, Dominique also made a classic mistake that teachers new to a syllabus or exam method commonly make: he marked the mock examinations generously, awarding marks when marks shouldn't really have been awarded.

Following this, Dominique did finally realize how important it was for his students to gain exposure to exam-style questions on a regular basis.

However, it took him almost a year and half to uncover the deepest secret of training advanced learners: *always mark harshly.*

Training Advanced Learners: Your Top Priorities

- Expose your students to past-examination papers and exam-style questions on a regular basis, right from the start of their course. These can usually be found on the exam board websites, inside textbooks, on accompanying textbooks CD's and even on the blog sites and VLE pages of teachers in other schools.

- Always use official marking schemes and examiner's reports to mark past-exam papers or sample papers. Never make up your own mark schemes, and try to involve the students in the assessment process as much as possible (e.g. by self or peer assessment).

- Always mark exam-style questions harshly! If you are unsure whether or not a student has gained a mark, then do not award it! This will train your students to be rigorous in their responses and it will reinforce the key vocabulary and methods required by the examination.

- Use peer-assessment often, but make sure that you go over the student work yourself to make sure that no misconceptions have been assumed. Try getting the students to come up with their own marking schemes, and let them see how these compare to the official ones provided by the exam board.

Secret Number 24: Know your coursework

Exam boards are increasingly including coursework as an assessed component of advanced level programmes. For some exam boards this is completely internally assessed, with samples of work being sent out of school for moderation. For others, all coursework is completely externally assessed, and still for others there is a mix of both internal and external assessment.

If you are new to a syllabus or exam board and you are unsure about how to pursue with the coursework elements, then *you must seek help*. Speak with your head of department or with colleagues who are teaching similar courses or who have taught your course before. You'll often find that subjects are grouped together by exam boards (e.g. humanities and sciences) and the coursework style and assessment method will be very similar, if not the same, for each subject. If you can't seek help within your school, then your exam board will publish teacher support materials which will often provide exhaustive explanations of the coursework procedures for your subject, with some even giving examples of student work that has been assessed for you to look at.

For some exam boards (such as the International Baccalaureate®), attending a training course can be a brilliant way for you to gain good quality knowledge of your subject's coursework requirements from other teachers who've been teaching the syllabus for years. However, these can be expensive, and if your school budget doesn't allow for this, then try networking with professionals in other schools nearby. Senior managers nearly always encourage inter-school collaboration, as it benefits students and staff. Failing that, you could try using your exam board's FAQ forums (such as the International Baccalaureate's Online Curriculum Centre), where you'll probably find that other teachers have had the same queries as you.

Knowing your coursework is absolutely essential in maximizing the success of your students. I've seen it all too often – teachers misunderstanding coursework requirements, causing their students to either be marked down by external moderators or to score poorly overall. Having a good handle on how best to manage your coursework requirements will provide you with the knowledge and skills you need to guide your students properly. It's the one area where they can gain marks before they sit the final examinations, so make sure it's done properly!

Coursework Beware: Common Internal Assessment Pitfalls

- Keep original student work in school, if your timetable allows the students to complete it all during lesson time. Students can lose work when they take it home, so make sure you've got backup copies – either as soft files (these are best) or photocopies.

- Train students to backup their work! I've dealt with too many students in the past who have corrupted their soft files and have no backup file to refer too. This type of error can be devastating, and can bring a student back to square one.

- If you are accepting soft-files from students, then watch out for nasty Apple/Microsoft interchange issues. Find out which types of file submission work best for all of the students in your class. I have personally found that it's best for students to save files as pdfs, since this avoids awkward page errors and unexpected file corruption.

- If your exam board allows, then always annotate coursework heavily before you send it off. Moderators are much less likely to mark your work down if they can actually see good justifications for the scores you've awarded to a student.

- Some exam boards will allow your students to submit a first draft before they complete a final version. You must find out if your exam board allows this, as it can dramatically affect the grades of your students. Don't just assume that because your colleagues do not accept a first draft that this must be an exam board regulation. Be absolutely sure! Check your syllabus and teacher support materials.

Secret number 25: Your students never really leave school

Have you ever bumped into one of your old students in a restaurant, shop, on public transport or in the street? I know that I have, on more occasions than I can count! The conversation usually begins with a "Hi! Wow, it's great to see you! What are you up to these days?"

We must always solemnly remember our number one duty as teachers when we are placed in a situation like this: that we need to be positive role-models for all of our students, whether or not they are current or former pupils of ours.

Whenever I suddenly meet with a former student of mine, I am still in my 'teacher frame of mind'. My key priorities for the conversation are as follows:

1. To find out how the person is and encourage them to talk about their current situation

2. To show them that I still care about their wellbeing, even though they are no longer my student

3. To find out about the positive things they are doing, or plan to do, in their life, and offer encouragement and advice

4. To get the person to think about their future ambitions

I'll always remember going along to a school reunion when I was a very energetic (and dumb) 23 year old. I'd just finished university, and I told my former teachers all about my life. I was proud to tell them that I had gotten my degree in Molecular Biology, especially when I spoke with my former science teachers. However, what was extra special that evening was the words of my former Physics teacher, Mr Wardle, who said "Richard, I'm so pleased that you've gotten your degree. You always did work hard in school, and it's clear that you're still working very hard", Wow! Now that felt really good! I still enjoyed receiving praise and encouragement from Mr Wardle, even though I hadn't seen him in years.

It was a very motivational sentence that he spoke to me, and I've always recognised its value whenever I meet one of my former students.

What does this have to do with classroom management? How does offering encouragement and guidance to former students help you with the classes you teach today? Well, the answer actually has three parts:

1. You develop a more advanced caring and nurturing mindset when you consistently take an interest in all of your students: even those who have left school. This mindset helps you to be more nurturing and caring with your current students.

2. A good conversation with a former student can really help you to see the 'end-game' of all of the education the student has gone through. I've met former students who've gone on to do master's degrees and PhDs, started businesses and others who have gone into the apprenticeship and employment market straight from school. All of these conversations have provided me with information and careers advice that I can pass on to my current students.

3. Many of your former students will be connected directly or indirectly to your current students and parents (even if you've changed location). When that 22 year old man who talked to you about his current degree studies talks to your current student or students, or their parents, you want him to say nice things about you and to feel empowered to move on to the next stage of his life (because, in that short conversation, you've encouraged and motivated him).

The Student's Perspective: An Interview with Jeffrey McLean

I interviewed Jeffrey McLean: a Year 13 (18 years old) IB Diploma student who attended an elite international school in Bangkok. As a 'pre-university' student, who has received seven years of secondary education, I wanted to find out what his take was on what makes a good lesson. Jeffrey's responses provide us with insights relating to good *lesson planning, effective teacher-student rapport* and array of *pointers for teaching advanced learners.*

So, I've got a few questions I'll ask you if that's okay. First of all, Jeff, you've been a high school student for seven years; so you've come to the end of your time in school. You'll never go back to high school as a student for the rest of your life. So you are an 'expert' on what makes a good teacher and what makes a bad teacher. Okay, because you've seen them all, I'm sure. I'm sure you've seen really good teachers, and I'm sure you've seen really bad teachers. So my question for you is, could you talk about some of the best lessons you've ever had over your time as a high school student?

I think one of the best lessons I ever had happened just recently. In my Geography class we were going over part of the core syllabus and as an exercise what we did is my teacher had some past paper questions cut up and we were put into groups and each group had to get through all of their past-paper questions within the time of the lesson. So it was kind of like a competition, but the teacher would look at your answer and judging on what you wrote he'd see if you'd be able to get past that question or not. So you had to get all the points on the mark scheme, in order to get to the next question. And so, it made us go through our books and see all the points that we had, and ones that we were missing and if we were missing a point we'd write that into our notes and we'd remember that for next time.

Fantastic. And how did the teacher show you the mark scheme exactly?

Jeff: He was sitting at a table with all the questions and model answers. We'd go up to him with our answers and he'd say 'you've got that point and that point correct, but you're missing something'

I see, I see. Wonderful. And can you think of anything, maybe when you were really young like in Year 7, or Year 8 or Year 9 that you particularly remember? Anything that kind of stands out?

For some reason I always remember this science class where we got to go outside and make paper airplanes and investigate how changing the dimensions of the wings affected their area. It wasn't very accurate but...

But it worked, yes? And that teacher who you were throwing the paper airplanes for; was that teacher a person who you felt you could relate with? Someone who you could talk to? Was that teacher someone who was quiet and who didn't connect well with students? What would you say?

Most of my teachers have been pretty friendly, and they've all been pretty approachable. I feel like if you can make a connection with a teacher, then you're much more likely to ask them a question that you're unsure about.

So being approachable is an important skill, you think, for a new teacher?

I think, even like pretending like you care about your students is important. You've got Year 7 students and Year 13 students who've got exams in a couple of days and even just pretending like their problems are important is good. It makes for a better learning experience for them.

That's good to hear. That's really good advice that, Jeff. Because I think what happens with a lot of students in schools is that, unfortunately, they feel as though they're just one of many and they don't feel as though they receive adequate individual attention sometimes. Okay, so, my next big question is what do you think a good lesson should contain?

Any good lesson will have several different activities and things to do, because I think most teenagers have a problem where their attention span isn't very long. So, if you do one thing for a prolonged period of time the students are less likely to remember the stuff at the end and in the middle. Because I think what some of my teachers used to say is that you're most likely to remember the first and the last things that you're told, and the stuff in the middle is what you're most likely to forget. So I guess if you're doing more than one activity, there's more starts and finishes. You're more likely to remember a greater volume of information.

That's a very good pedagogical summary, Jeff. You know, funnily enough, my first ever teacher-training session at Bangor University all those years ago, the first thing my tutor said was 'a good lesson should contain a lot of variety'. So you have said the same as a PhD tutor at a top university. So it just goes to show that the student experience matches the expert's advice. My next question is, could you describe some of your favourite teachers to me?

I think a theme that is shared between all of my good teachers is that they all have a good sense of humour. Because most of my classes at school are small, it's easy to make a connection with the teachers. So, the personality traits that they would have is that ... One of the teachers that I really like engages in just normal chit-chat with the students, before and after class, and he makes us feel like he actually cares about us, in a classroom setting. He a friendly teacher.

So he's friendly, and you get the impression that he's not just there to teach you a subject but that he actually cares about what's happening?

I guess it's more like he treats us like we're adults, not children. So I guess he kind of has to be helpful . He'll stop in the hall and ask us 'what are you having for lunch today?'

So he has a good relationship there. And you mentioned a good sense of humour before. What does that mean to you; when a teacher has a good sense of humour? Can you think of any examples? Because that's a problem that a lot of teachers have. Many teachers don't gauge humour correctly, I mean, I'm even guilty of that sometimes. So what would you say a good sense of humour for a teacher is?

I think a good sense of humour is one that, I kind of feel bad saying this, but, the teachers know which students they can pick on. Which students will understand the jokes that they make, and it's kind of like some students when they're made fun of they don't take it the same way as others, because they expect their teachers to be a bit more formal than that. But then, I think, being a bit less formal is also good for building a good relationship with students.

Can you think of an example where a teacher has done something really funny and has kind of got everyone on track, or something like that?

In my biology class there are two girls who have trouble with their pronunciation of words. So when they say something outrageous, the teacher will take a second and try to get us to help them to correct their pronunciation. And sometimes he even goes online to find the British and American ways to say a word. So I guess it's educational but it's also funny because we get to have a laugh about people not being able to say words and they're good about that. And also, just thinking about the word for prolonged periods of time makes it stick in your head a bit more. Oh, and I've just thought of something that one of my teachers does that is funny. He's not afraid to make a fool out of himself. In my geography class there's lots of global issues that we deal with. And my teacher always goes back to Michael Jackson and healing the world and stuff. So, often he'll play a song over the speaker system in the class and he'll sing along with it. It's nice for like a break from the class but it's also really funny because we get to see our teacher make a fool out of himself.

I see. That's quite an advanced technique that, isn't it, because he's using the pronunciation as a kind way of showing sympathy for the girls who couldn't pronounce the word correctly and he's reinforcing that key piece of terminology as well. Also, your geography teacher uses song to make the lesson memorable. So that's quite impressive actually. Those are good examples to share. Okay, so my next question is what advice would you give to a teacher who is new to the profession?

It's kind of difficult because in Canada I used to go to a public school and the advice you would give to a public school teacher and a private school teacher is probably different. I think for a public school teacher I'd probably say to have a structured class environment and take your role as somebody who should be the leader of a class. But then in a private school maybe I'd give all the students in the class the attention they deserve because everybody likes positive attention.

I see. So why do you suggest this difference between a public and private school approach?

I think public school students are more likely to act up. I think public school classes are usually a bit bigger, whereas private school classes are a bit smaller so you have less stuff to worry about in a private school than you do in a public school.

I see. Have you ever been in a class in a public school where you've had students act up around you?

Yes. About two years ago I went back to the high school that I would I have went to in Canada. Seeing the difference between my school and this school in Canada. The teacher didn't really have full control over the class, so all of the activities that he tried to do seemed to take a lot longer than he'd planned, and the kids would have to stay after class and stuff like that. Just because there were a couple of students who didn't have the discipline that others did.

I see. And how do you think that that teacher could have put the discipline into that class?

I think if they'd established that were a teacher that has limits from the start that'd help. Also having a system where if a student does something bad they get punished, and where if a student does something good they get rewarded would help. Because sometimes if all that happens is that you het told off when you're doing something wrong, and you never get told when you're doing something right, it's not good because you want that feeling of achievement.

Which subjects do you enjoy the most at school?

I only take six subjects, but I enjoy five of them a lot. I like French, Math, Geography and Biology the most, then Chemistry and English last.

Do you think you enjoy those five subjects because of the way they are taught, or because of the subjects themselves?

Probably the way they've been taught. I started Year 12 not liking Math at all.

Yes, talk to me about that. What happened to get you from not liking Math in Year 12 to liking Math now?

Seeing my progression over time. Seeing my development as a student. I think looking back on my test scores and seeing how I've improved and seeing which revision techniques worked best for me. Like in Math it's pretty straight forward; if you do lots of questions to practice, you'll get better at it. As I learned that, Math became more and more enjoyable for me because I could see my improvements and I'd strive for that more because in a subject that I struggled with, getting a 6 or a 7 made me want to try harder for next time.

So you saw yourself getting better and that motivated you to move forward. Do you think the teacher deliberately made things hard at the start or do you think that was just normal?

I actually think that he did do that.

I see. What makes you think that?

I think because at the start of Year 13 I started scoring very highly. On both of my reports this year I got a level 7 for Math, whereas last year I got a 4 and a 6. So maybe he started the course very difficult, so that the people who would drop down to do Maths Studies would do it then and there. This allowed him to have a serious class for the rest of the year.

I see. And at any time when your teacher was making life really hard for you, did you think of quitting and moving down to Maths Studies yourself?

There wasn't really any time that I thought about that because I feel like (Math) Studies is pretty limiting, especially when you look at the number of universities that don't accept students with Math Studies.

Reflection time!

1. What does this interview teach us about the importance of teacher behaviours in motivating students to learn?

2. What did we learn about the subliminal cues that Jeffrey up from his teachers as he progressed through high school?

3. What can we, as teachers, take from this interview to make us better practitioners?

Teaching Advanced Learners: Summary

Teaching older students can be a very fulfilling and exciting experience. The challenge of covering complex subject material, along with training students for exams, provides teachers with cumulative experience that prepares them well for a long and fruitful career. Make sure that you never lose sight of these important nuggets of advice:

- Know your course: always teach the correct syllabus (you'd be surprised at how many teachers don't). Make sure that students have access to the syllabus, and that all lesson content matches the course outcomes as specified by the exam board.

- The clock is always ticking: aim to get your syllabus finished a few weeks before the terminal exams (at the latest). Include a focused revision period on the run up to the finals, and make sure you are using past-exam papers as part of the revision process.

- Advanced learners are not always 'advanced': even older students can, and will, behave like small children. Don't let up on your vigilance and professionalism, and always make sure that standards are high. Do not allow poor performance to go unchecked, and use your school's rewards and sanctions system correctly.

- Subject knowledge does not always equate to good teaching. Equip your students with the skills they need to be independent learners by allowing them to discover answers for themselves. Allow opportunities for intellectual collaboration, and make sure that you know enough about the subject to prompt the investigative process.

- Train your students to pass the exam. Make sure that you expose your students to exam-style questions often, and get them involved in the assessment process. Remember to always mark harshly!

- Do you need to really 'predict' grades? Find out what your school specifically means by 'predicted grades' and make sure that you are assessing your students regularly, using exam-style questions. Use assessment data as your basis for making realistic predictions.

- Understand the 'ins and outs' of your subject's coursework. Read through the official exam board website, teacher support materials and syllabus carefully. Consult your colleagues in your school and in other schools for advice. Keep student work organized and always make sure that you have backup copies.

CHAPTER 5

Using ICT to enhance learning: Training students to embrace the robotic age

"When faced with a steam-rolling technology, you either become part of the technology or part of the road!"

Nigel Willets (ICT Teacher and columnist for www.ictineducation.org)

In my relatively short lifetime on this planet (32 years at the time of writing), I have witnessed phenomenal change in the way that Information and Communication Technology (ICT) is used in classrooms. As a primary school student I was lucky to get a chance to play games on an old BBC computer, and that was only if I was a good boy that day! In high school, through the mid-to-late 90's and the early part of this century, I progressed from using old Acorn™ computers in GCSE IT lessons to finally typing in my first keyword search on Google™ when I was 16. At university my lecturers were forward-thinking enough to really embrace ICT by sharing their presentations and learning resources through websites, blogs and e-mail. Many of my friends in other universities were not lucky enough to experience this.

In my time as a high school teacher of mathematics and science, I have had to constantly learn the 'ins and outs' of new ICT systems in order to help my students to learn material effectively, and to meet the requirements of senior management and school inspectors! It goes without saying: **high school teachers today need to be as pliable as a spring when it comes to utilizing new technology to aid the learning process.**

This can be a challenge for many stakeholders in today's schools. On the one hand, school management may welcome the use of ICT in as many lessons as possible, but may not be able to provide the funds to purchase new hardware, software and training for staff and parents. From the teacher's point of view, it can be frustrating when one system has been used for a short period of time, only to be scrapped or replaced with something new. Additionally, the advent of Virtual Learning Environments (VLE's) such as Moodle™, Firefly™ and Edmodo™ has meant that, in the schools that use these, our teaching strategies and approaches have become more transparent than ever before. We can no longer hide behind the classroom door, confident in the knowledge that our lessons aren't being observed. When you use a VLE properly, every teacher in your school can view your resources and can figure out your programme of study for each class you teach.

This can be intimidating, especially when those one or two tech-savvy teachers are doing amazing things with their websites, blogs and subject pages, and you've got something that seems poor in comparison. However, don't fret! We're going to hit this problem right on the head, and obliterate it for all eternity!

My aims for this chapter are primarily as follows:

- To get you to think about ways in which you can use technology to enhance your teaching

- To share with you the many strategies that have worked for me and others when trying to engage students through technology

- To encourage you to adopt a 'growth mindset', along with a genuine interest and excitement for working with ICT systems.

- To show you how to get the students to generate much of the technological outputs that come from learning, bypassing the need for the teacher to 'know everything'.

I am a realist. I know that the strategies that have worked for me and others (and which I'll share with you in this chapter) will one day be out of date. We are on the cusp of a trans-humanist, robotic age where the future would seem to resemble vividly the world portrayed by Philip K. Dick's *The Minority Report*. We are all going to have to learn how to use new technology in the future, both personally and for our jobs as teachers. Let's do the sensible thing and welcome this, as opposed to being an old grouch and complaining, like one of my former colleagues, by saying "Teachers didn't need to do all of this when I was a student, and look at me now!". This mindset is still, unfortunately, rather commonplace. As teachers, we have to realise that education has changed and will keep changing at an ever increasing pace. Sooner or later we're all going to have to embrace these exciting changes.

The good news is that using ICT in the classroom doesn't need to be difficult, and you don't necessarily need to have done a lot of training or preparation before using a particular system or strategy. In fact, if used properly, new technology can actually relieve the teacher of doing lots of 'mundane' tasks such as marking, printing and even actual teaching! That's right; ICT systems are slowly replacing the need for teachers to even deliver content to their students! As computers take over our classrooms and learning spaces, teachers are becoming more like *facilitators* rather than *deliverers* of knowledge. This is an exciting time to be an educator, and I hope that this chapter will show you just how much fun it can be to implement technology into your teaching.

Secret number 25: Make Good Use of Smart Phones and Tablets

I can still remember the first day I owned a mobile phone. I was 16 years old, I'd just finished my GCSE exams, and my parents bought me a classic Philips 'brick' phone with a pointy aerial and a cool bleep tone when I received an SMS. I thought it was the coolest thing on Earth. Unfortunately, my teachers were not so enthusiastic about this new technology.

It wasn't long before my teachers were confiscating phones from my peers left, right and centre. This trend continued when I started my career as a teacher in 2006, and it was always a very unpleasant (and confrontational) experience whenever I saw a pupil with a mobile phone in hand and I was duty-bound to confiscate it because of school policy. Now, finally, after a very long wait, teachers are starting to see the benefits of using mobile phones to assist in a wide-variety of learning activities.

What follows next is a breakdown of the smart phone activities that I and my colleagues have used to make learning interactive, fun and meaningful. You may be able to think of more ideas than what's listed here and, by the time this book is published, there will no doubt be a new app or device that can enhance learning in ways that I haven't mentioned here.

Don't be camera shy!

Smart phone cameras are absolutely amazing learning tools as they can often double up as scanners, analysers and editors when paired with the correct app or software programme. When used properly, they can get students out of the classroom and can act as conduits for engaging the 'whole brain'.

That being said, one does have to be quite cautious when using smart phone cameras with students. There are many documented cases of pupils filming their friends or teachers covertly in school, and then instantly sharing the footage via social media or even video-sharing sites such as YouTube™. In schools and countries where there are heavy child-protection laws and policies, this can be quite serious and can land the supervising teacher in a lot of trouble. My approach to this problem has always been to lay down the ground rules with my students first (i.e. to only use their cameras for the task at hand), and then make sure I am vigilant in supervising the activity. If you do this, then smart phone camera activities will be an enjoyable part of your teaching, and will greatly enhance the students' learning experiences.

Smart phone savvy: camera-based learning activities:

1. *Code scanning treasure hunts*: This activity involves getting the students to scan codes (e.g. QR codes) using their smart phones and then following the clues to find information. It involves some planning and preparation by the teacher beforehand, but it is well worth it!

The steps to follow are:

- *Step 1*: Create a sequence of information sheets (e.g. five sheets of information about different aspects of cell division)

- *Step 2*: Insert a QR code (or other) into each sheet. QR codes can be created for free at www.qrstuff.com. Your QR codes should encode a clue to tell the students where to go (e.g. 'Go to the library' or 'This is where you eat fish and chips on a Friday')

- *Step 3*: Hide your clues in different places around the school (try to use rooms and places that will be unoccupied, if possible). Make sure your first information sheet (with an embedded QR code clue) is in the classroom where you will start!

- *Step 4:* Make sure that all of the students have the 'QR Reader' app (or similar) installed on their smart phones. This can be set as homework before the lesson starts, to save time.

- *Step 5*: The students will scan the codes and follow the clues, picking up the information sheets as they race or walk around the school.

- When the students have picked up all the information sheets (the last QR code 'clue' should be something like 'Go back to class'), then the students will come back to their classroom and complete an activity with the sheets. You may wish for them to organize the information in some way (e.g. into a poster or flowchart, which can be used in a fun memory game like the 'Poster Game' – covered in chapter two). You could also get the students to communicate the information in an unusual way (e.g. by texting a friend or by posting to the school's blog via their smart phone)

  You can also use code-scanning in other inventive ways too, such as linking students to a particular website or connecting them to a Dropbox™ account so that they can submit work electronically. You can use as many clues as you want (I usually find that between five and seven works well).

2. *Creating stop-motion animations*: This is a particularly good activity for helping the students to learn about a particular process or sequence (e.g. the events leading up to the Second World War). A stop-motion animation is basically where the students take a series of photographs (e.g. of a model being made, or figurines being moved into position) and then movie-maker software is used to string the photographs along in a fluid sequence. There are a series of apps (for free) that students can use to make these on their iPads™ and iPhones™, including Stop Motion Studio™, iMotion™ and FlipBook™. There are also a variety of apps available for the Android™ platform too.

ICT in the Classroom: Using Smart Phones and Tablets to Scan Codes
By Richard James Rogers @richardjarogers

Here are two 'clues' from a real treasure hunt that I recently did with my IBDP Year 13 Biology class:

This tells me (the teacher) where to actually put the clue. This is really important because you can confuse yourself, especially if it is a big treasure hunt with a lot of clues

This tells me and the students which group the clue is for. If you have a really small class (e.g. four or five students), then you may wish to send them all off as one group. With larger classes, it can be good to have many groups hunting for different clues around the school.

Classroom Group 1

Staffroom group 1

Lactose is the sugar found in milk. It can be broken down by the enzyme lactase into glucose and galactose. However, some people lack this enzyme and so cannot break down lactose. This leads to lactose intolerance. Lactose intolerant people need to drink milk that has been lactose reduced.

Lactose-free milk can be made in two ways. The first involves adding the enzyme lactase to the milk so that the milk contains the enzyme. The second way involves immobilizing the enzyme on a surface or in beads of a porous material. The milk is then allowed to flow past the beads or surface with the immobilized lactase. This method avoids having lactase in the milk.

This is a QR code created for free at qrstuff.com

This tells the students where to go next

Try scanning this code for yourself

Substrate
Active Site
Enzyme

Students use a QR Reader app to scan the codes

This is a place where your cool teachers hang out and talk about their amazing students!

Once the QR code hunt has finished you can get the kids to arrange the information in specific way (e.g. as a flow chart, poster or leaflet) or you can get them to complete a project based on it (e.g. making a movie)

The only disadvantage I've found with this activity is that it does take some time to complete. You may wish to run this over a series of lessons, or start it in class and then set it as a homework activity.

3. *Record and edit videos*: A nice project-based piece of work for students of any high school age is to make videos that illustrate a concept or which demonstrate understanding of content. This works especially well when done as a group activity, providing lots of scope for creative freedom (which students love). There are a wide variety of apps available that crop videos and which add music, text, animations and special effects. I've used this activity many times with both advanced learners and younger students. The only real downside is that the finished movies can vary in quality of you don't make the learning outcomes really clear to the students from the start. Overall, however, this is a great activity and you don't even need to know how to make smart phone movies yourself – the students can be tasked with finding this out for themselves (although you may want to suggest some apps they could use beforehand).

4. *Portable homework diary*: Are you sick of your students forgetting their homework? Does your school still use those old-fashioned homework diaries where everything needs to be written down? If you're school isn't using a homework database or a VLE to set assignments, then one way to solve this is to get the students to take a photograph of the homework task after you've written it on the whiteboard or projected it. This is also a very good option for students with additional learning needs and those who are operating with English as their second language. Additionally, if the homework is complex and involves multiple steps (e.g. navigating through a particular VLE portal), then students should be encouraged to take photographs of each step in the process.

5. ***Meme generator***: A meme is a funny picture with a sentence or two above and below the main image. Students can use their camera to take their own images, or can simply use those provided by free apps such as 'MemeCreator' and 'Meme Producer' (Apple™) and 'Best Meme Generator' and 'Free Meme Generator' (Android™). Once the memes have been created, they can be tweeted to a class hashtag, shared on the class blog or even turned into a set of revision notes or a presentation. They offer a fun and creative way for students to generate statements of their understanding of subject content, and can therefore be a useful way for you to check if what your teaching is being understood properly!

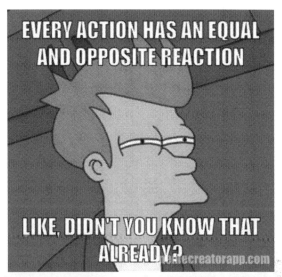

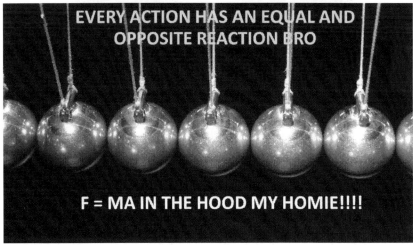

Examples of memes that my students have created using their smart phones. As you can see, the students can take a photo using their smart phone camera, or they can use one of a range of images provided by the various meme creation apps.

6. *Magazine cover*: There are various apps available on both smart phones and tablets that allow you to create a magazine or newspaper front cover. These can act as great summaries, and students can take photographs straight from their device to do this. Short statements can be used as topic or concept summaries, offering a fun revision tool. Additionally, students can go online without using an app and can actually create a magazine cover using an interactive wizard. My favourite site for this is http://bighugelabs.com/magazine.php, as this site allows you to edit the title, text and background image in a matter of seconds. If the students use their own images, or pictures with no attribution (e.g. as found on www.pixabay.com), then they can even share their work on social media sites and the school's VLE. An example of a student-generated magazine cover is shown on page 138.

The six activities I've mentioned already are my personal favourites when it comes to using smart phone or tablet cameras in lessons. However, the scope for using handhelds in teaching is absolutely enormous, and some other ideas you may wish to consider (and which have worked well for me) are as follows:

General activities involving smart phones and tablets

- *Scheduling homework through various calendars*: These will update automatically if the students have a school e-mail address that's linked to a platform such as Microsoft Office 365™ or Google Calendar™. It's worth making sure that all of your students (particularly advanced learners) have their school e-mail system set up on their smart phone or tablet, and that the relevant calendars are switched on. This can have a huge advantage over using a VLE to set homework, as the students will receive a calendar alert on their device when homework is due in. Speak to your school's ICT administrator to see if this is possible for your classes.

- ***Producing graphs for project-based work***: Any form of data set can be graphed in various ways by tablets and smart phones. This could happen in a history lesson in which you're studying the number of new cases of the bubonic plaque over a set period of time; a mathematics lesson where the students have conducted a simple survey; a science lesson where the kids are measuring the light absorbance of different solutions or even an English lesson where you're studying the frequency of particular adjectives in different texts. Good graphing apps include 'Numbers', 'Viz', '3D Charts' and 'Chart Maker' (Apple™) and 'Simple Graph Maker', 'My Graph (Chart)', 'ChartGo' and 'Juice Labs' (Android™).

Mutants Daily

The Mutant Monthly Digest

DNA: CONTAINS 4 BASES
A BINDS WITH T

C BINDS WITH G
mRNA - Fully Spliced!

CYSTIC FIBROSIS
CAUSED BY AN INHERITED MUTATION

BEST MUTAGEN
PARAQUAT VS. OZONE

June 30th 2014
THB 300

0 71361 06121 7

A magazine front cover created by one of my Year 12 Biology students. You'll notice that some sophisticated short phrases are included, which acted as 'memory joggers' when the students in the class used this for revision. Additionally, in the feedback process, this magazine cover gave me lots of prompts I could use to ask the student about the meaning of her work. Very subtly, she had changed a 'Daily' title to a 'Monthly' subtitle, explaining that this had been caused by a "frameshift mutation" – her exact words. She went on to explain all of the concepts covered by this work, elaborating in quite impressive detail

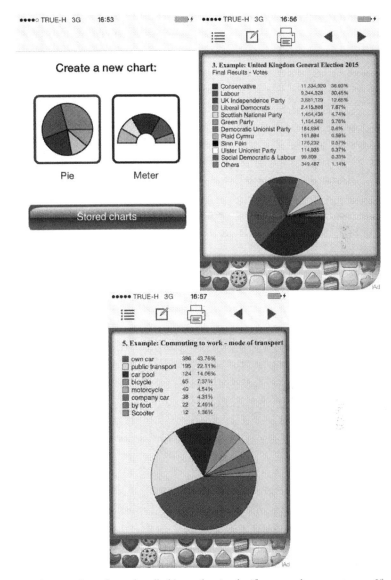

Creating charts and graphs on handhelds can be simple, if you use the correct apps. If your school has bookable tablets, then make sure that your ICT administrator installs the apps you want on all of the school's devices.

- *Clickers*: You can convert smart phones into classroom 'clickers' that can answer multiple-choice questions. Apps like ResponseWare™ (Apple™ and Android™) allow participants to respond to any interactive question using any web-enabled device. Apps like these require limited time to set up, but they can be costly. However, it's worth using some of your school's budget to invest in 'clickable' MCQ software, as it can provide teachers with a very quick snapshot of whole-class understanding, on a frequent basis. They can be set so that each participant is anonymous, making the students feel more at ease with submitting a response.

- *Voice-commanded research*: Some students (especially those with special educational needs) do prefer to do research via voice command rather than by typing on a small screen. Thankfully, modern smart phones automatically have this feature built in, and can provide answers to questions or commands in seconds. This will work with the simple phone microphone, hands free kit or Bluetooth™ headset. It's important that the student speaks slowly and clearly, keeping the number of words to a minimum. A good command would be "Tell me the time in Brazil" as opposed to "I would be very grateful if you could please tell me what time it is now in Brazil". One thing to be careful about is whether or not the device is using Siri™ (Apple) or Voice Control. Make sure the phone is configured correctly beforehand by doing a quick test, otherwise you might find the student 'dialing' numbers through voice control unintentionally! If students are using their own phones, then they'll probably already know how to do this properly.

- *Watching videos*: Any kind of project-based work that involves research lends itself very well to videos. Students are now turning to short video clips as a quick and more stimulating alternative to reading through reams of text (much of which may be irrelevant, especially if it's contained in a non-subject/exam board connected website). Whilst YouTube™ is still the most popular video hosting website on the web, there are a number of good alternatives, including:

  o *Vimeo*: This a fast-growing platform with a lot of traffic. Unlike YouTube, Vimeo mostly holds professional-looking videos and has two options for its users: a basic account with restrictions and a paid one (which has advanced options and bigger space).

  o *Dailymotion*: This is a French video-sharing website that allows users to view videos by searching tags, channels or user-created groups. Students can also upload videos here too, if that is part of their project.

  o *Veoh*: This is an Internet television service that hosts independent productions, studio-generated content and other user-produced material. Veoh probably lends itself better to video sharing as opposed to video viewing, as it allows students to upload videos of any length and embed them on their (or the school's) website, VLE or blog. Veoh accepts hundreds of different formats and is very user-friendly.

One thing to note about students watching videos – make sure they are wearing earphones and that the volume is not excessive! A class full of students watching videos and listening to the sound through speakers can quickly degenerate into an unpleasant and distracting environment.

- *Creating, uploading and sharing videos*: The vast majority of high school students these days are very creative and have had much more exposure to different computer systems than us teachers did at their age and younger. Most students jump at the opportunity to make a video, and will be ecstatic if you allow them to share it too. However, do be careful with this one. Check what your school's stance is on sharing videos, and make sure you're vigilant in your role as teacher and check all content thoroughly before allowing the students to share it. Generally, videos that do not actually feature the students themselves (such as animations or academic, text-based presentations) are fine to share anywhere. However, you have to be more careful when the students are actually featured in the videos, especially if they are young teenagers. We will examine the safe use of ICT in teaching later on, but what I will say here is that for any type of 'sharing', it's always best to keep the original content only on school devices, and share only on school-approved platforms such as your VLE or class blog. Always double-check with your school administrators if you are unsure.

- **Peer Assessment**: One of the best time-saving ways that technology can be used in teaching is for the peer-assessment of student work. If this is done properly, then good quality, unbiased feedback can be provided to each student and this will save you spending hours out of your weekends and evenings writing long comments on assignments. Sounds great, doesn't it? But how does it work?

You can have students peer-assess their friends' essays through a Google Form embedded on a teacher page, and allow them to view real-time constructive criticism. The steps to follow are:

1. Get your students to send you their work via e-mail or through your school's VLE

2. Remove the student name from the work and add an unique user ID of your choosing (making the work anonymous)

3. Send each student's work to a different student

4. Go into Google Drive and create a new form (e.g. a form containing questions about the work the student has viewed)

5. Add collaborators (other teachers, if you wish)

6. Edit each question type by entering the question, adding help text, choosing the question type (there are nine different types) and if the question is mandatory, you can check the 'Required question' box

7. Insert images, videos, page and section breaks (if required)

8. Choose what happens after a student submits the form (e.g. by displaying a confirmation message or providing a link to another website)

9. Choose the way that users (your students) will access and submit the form. You may wish to get the students to login with a Google Apps account, or submit the form anonymously. You can also choose to shuffle the questions.

10. Choose the colour and style of your form. Google offer a number of themes for you to choose from.

11. Choose where the form data will be saved. Make sure you check the box that says 'Always create a new spreadsheet'.

12. Send out the form to your students. This can be done via e-mail, or by sharing a link (e.g. on your school's website, VLE or your class blog). You can also insert the link into a document.

13. The students will fill in the form and submit their responses

14. Once you have received the responses, Google Drive will store all of the data into a spreadsheet. It's often necessary to polish this up a little before sharing it with the students. Believe me, this is worth it, because the students will be really interested to see the results of the entire class altogether.

15. Make sure that you share each individual response with each student it pertains to. As part of the feedback process, you should sit with each student and talk about the responses they got. As with all peer-assessment, if it's guided properly it can offer good quality feedback, but misconceptions can also arise. Your job as a teacher is to clear up these misconceptions as they arise, and to make sure that the student understands and acts on their feedback.

If you're having problems creating Google forms then don't panic, because there's lots of very good help available online. For more guidance, look up Eric Curts' 'Using Google Forms' and Tom Barret's excellent presentation entitled '81 Ways Teachers Can Use Google Forms With Their Students'

A good Google Form for students will look something like this:

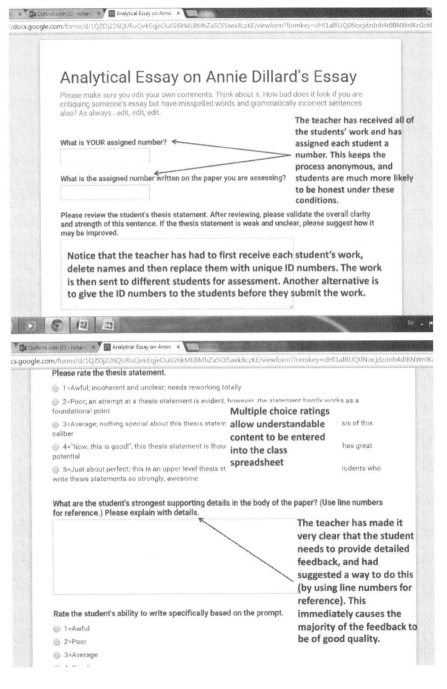

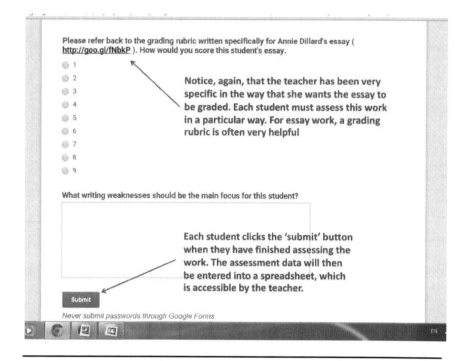

Please refer back to the grading rubric written specifically for Annie Dillard's essay (http://goo.gl/fNbkP). How would you score this student's essay.

○ 1
○ 2
○ 3
○ 4
○ 5
○ 6
○ 7
○ 8
○ 9

Notice, again, that the teacher has been very specific in the way that she wants the essay to be graded. Each student must assess this work in a particular way. For essay work, a grading rubric is often very helpful

What writing weaknesses should be the main focus for this student?

Each student clicks the 'submit' button when they have finished assessing the work. The assessment data will then be entered into a spreadsheet, which is accessible by the teacher.

Submit

Never submit passwords through Google Forms

#Edutechdebate: Tablets vs. Smart Phones in Education

- Every smart phone teaching technique that I've suggested can almost always be used with tablets too

- Tablets do provide a larger screen and greater accessibility to some programs and simulations, and this is a big advantage for students who like large text and who have issues with manual dexterity

- Always test the software first: Unfortunately, many programs and simulations that work on a Windows™ PC do not function properly on tablets and smart phones that use other operating systems. It's really embarrassing and frustrating to set a wonderful ICT-based learning task only to discover that it isn't compatible with the kids' devices.

- If you're planning on getting students to submit docs, PowerPoints or pdf files through Dropbox, or if you want students to download a file of this type, then tablets are typically better than smart phones. The larger screen means that more readable text can be displayed on the screen, and this also makes it much easier to edit files.

- Cost is an important factor when considering ICT orders in schools. Tablets generally cost two to three times less than their smart phone counterparts, and often allow for greater functionality. The other advantage is that school tablets will have been set up consistently by an ICT administrator, and will often not have SIM cards that connect them to a cellular network. This means that kids are much less likely to be playing around on social media when using school tablets, since sites like Facebook™, Instagram™ and others are much more difficult to access without their corresponding apps. Schools can also put controls in place to prevent access to such platforms.

- One downside of tablets is that they can be slow, especially if multiple students are using them to access the internet via the school's Wi-Fi system all at the same time. Smartphones can offer a quicker alternative in these cases.

- Students are much more likely to share school tablets with each other, rather than sharing their highly personalized smart phones with their peers. This has obvious ramifications for group work.

- One big advantage of tablets is that their battery life tends to be much longer than that of smart phones. Your school's set should also be regularly charged by the ICT administrator.

Secret Number 26: If your school has ICT labs, then use them!

One moment in my early days of teaching that I remember very vividly was when I was asked to substitute for another teacher one morning in 2007. The Year 11 class that I was asked to cover was infamous for being 'a disruptive group' in which there were a number of 'difficult students'. Whilst I didn't normally teach this class, I had listened to many rants and complaints from my colleagues about the students in this class who "just wouldn't listen" or who were "hyperactive".

The first thing I did upon receiving my cover instructions was to check if the ICT lab was available. I was lucky that day, because it was! As the students entered the computer suite, the look on their faces said "Yes! We're using the computers today!". Their task was to continue working on their GCSE coursework and with access to word processing, spreadsheet and desktop publishing software, they went right ahead and worked with no fuss at all!

At the end of the lesson my Head of Science at that time said something to me that made me very happy, and that I'll never forget. He said "Well done Richard, you did well with that class. If I'd have given this cover lesson to any other teacher, then they would have had problems". Wow! Now that felt good!

However, upon reflection, I think it was the ICT lab that actually saved the day and not me! Yes, it was true that I had a good rapport with almost all of the students in the school (even those that I didn't teach), because I consistently used the techniques outlined in chapter 1. However, since I didn't teach this class on a regular basis, I hadn't really had time to get to know these students properly (incidentally, however, because I taught their friends in other classes, they already had an idea of what I was like as a person because of what they had been told by their peers). Booking the ICT lab that day allowed me to instantly direct the students' attention *to their work*, whilst being able to walk around the class and help out with any technical issues the kids had. To be totally honest, I think I would probably have had 'problems' with that class that day if I was trying to teach them in a conventional classroom, especially since I had little knowledge of how much coursework each student had completed up until that point.

Almost all of the activities one can do on a tablet or smart phone (apart from mobile camera-dependant tasks, and some messaging activities) can also be completed on a conventional PC or laptop computer. Additionally, some big advantages of using a computer suite are that the screen size will typically be larger than a tablet or smart phone and internet connectivity is usually faster than it would be if cellular networks or Wi-Fi were being used instead of the school's landline. It's also easier to print under these conditions, and school computers should already have the basic office software you need pre-installed for you.

Secret Number 27: Social media can be used in teaching

Go back two or three years ago, and the thought of using any kind of social media in lessons was still very taboo in most schools. Now, however, a growing number of high schools are seeing the benefits that platforms such as Facebook™, Twitter™ and Instagram™ can bring to the classroom. Whilst all of this is very exciting, and very 'modern', we still have to tread very carefully. Some golden rules that we must follow as teachers when using social media with our students are as follows:

1. Always make sure that your students are of the permitted age to use the platform

2. Always show the students how to delete their account if needs be, and how to turn off notifications (some students and parents get very annoyed when they're constantly receiving e-mail updates from whichever social media platform it is that they've signed up to)

3. Remind your students of the SMART acronym:

    *   ***Stay Safe***: Don't give out your personal information to people or places you don't know

- ***Don't Meet Up***: It can be dangerous to meet up with someone you've only been in touch with online. Always check with an adult first

- ***Accepting Files***: Accepting images, e-mails, files or messages from people you don't know can cause problems

- ***Reliable***: Is the website or person telling the truth? Always check information before you believe it.

- ***Tell Someone***: Always inform an adult if someone or something online makes you feel uncomfortable or worried

If you follow these guidelines, then social media can offer a wealth of excitement, enrichment and interest to your lessons. It can encourage students to produce rich content, and can be examined instantly in a whole-class context.

Secret number 28: Train Kids to Train Themselves

The future uses of ICT in education require a wild imagination to visualise, and even then we probably won't be close to reality. Within a decade (easily), students will be using a range of cool interfaces to learn new information and skills. These may include:

- 3D holographic outputs which can be changed with a simple swipe of the hand

- Virtual reality simulators and headsets which build on Google Glass technology

- Robots and drones, and the ability to encode and work with artificial intelligence

- Hacking: Some primary school curricula now include cryptography and cryptanalysis in their programmes of study

- Microchip implants which allow for verification and interaction with a range of peripheral devices. The famous Defense

Advanced Research Projects Agency (DARPA) is currently working on a range of microchip implant technologies. One project, dubbed 'Systems of Neuromorphic Adaptive Plastic Scalable Electronics' (SyNAPSE), aims to develop "low-power electronic neuromorphic computers that scale to biological levels"[5]

- The ability to upload information directly to DNA (this is not science fiction - A bioengineer and a geneticist at Harvard's Wyss Institute have worked together to successfully store around 700 terabytes of information in a single gram of DNA[6]). Some logical follow-on research from this would be that which focuses on storing digital information directly in the brain, removing the need for 'learning' completely.

- A much wider range of voice-control interfaces than are used at present

[5] Defense Advanced Research Projects Agency (2015) [Online] Available from: http://www.darpa.mil/program/systems-of-neuromorphic-adaptive-plastic-scalable-electronics [Accessed: 18th October 2015]

[6] Alan Leo R. (2012). Harvard Medical School. *Writing the Book in DNA* [Online] Available from: http://hms.harvard.edu/news/writing-book-dna-8-16-12 [Accessed: 18th October 2015]

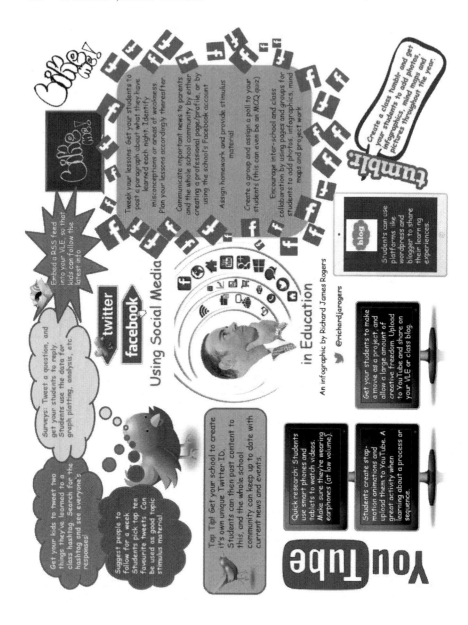

- Autonomous vehicles, such as the Google Self-Driving Car and AI-enabled drones. Google themselves predict that this technology could be made available to the general public by 2020[7].

[7] Rogers, C. 2015. The Wall Street Journal. Google Sees Self-Driving Car on Road Within Five Years [Online] Available from: http://www.wsj.com/articles/google-sees-self-drive-car-on-road-within-five-years-1421267677 [Accessed 17th September 2015]

The basic message that permeates all of these potential applications of future technology is simple: the world is changing, and it's changing fast! As educators, the only way that we can prepare our students for this is to **teach them how to teach themselves**. When our students are our age, they shall be using technologies that haven't even been invented yet, and they shall be working with concepts and knowledge that are not fully understood at this present moment.

So, the next time you ask your class to make a movie, or promote an event through social media, get them to figure out how to do it! Train your students to find the technological solutions to their problems and praise them when they do a good job. Provide feedback that's constructive and get your students to evaluate their methods. What could they have done if they'd have had more time? Did any technology hinder their progress? What kind of technology (real or imaginary) would have helped? The following worksheet may help with this process.

Using New Technology: Planning and Review Form

Name of person completing this form:
What is the task that you have been given?
Date:

Plan of action

Which technology (software and hardware) are you going to use for this project?
Which technology are you currently unfamiliar with? Where are you going to seek help?:
How are you going to use the technology (hardware and software) that you've listed?

If you are working in a group, then who will do what?

Evaluation of the task

Name of the person completing this form:	*Date:*
What was the task you were given?	

Follow Up Action

Now evaluate this task. You should think about the following:

- *How did you and your team approach this problem? Was this a good plan?*

- *Which pieces of technology worked well?*

- *Were there any 'bugs' or 'frustrations' with using any particular piece of technology?*

- *If you were to try this task again, which technology would you like to use (real or imaginary)?*

- *Did technology help you to complete this project, or did it make things more complicated?*

- *Were you pleased with your output? Why?*

- *What advice would you give to another student who's about to start this project?*

Summary: Using ICT to Enhance Learning

- Adopt a 'growth mindset' and be eager to see new ICT systems, technology and software as valuable educational tools. Take on the responsibility of keeping up to date with developments in educational technology and don't be afraid of trying something new.

- Include activities in your lessons in which students can use smart phones, tablets, smart watches and other mobile technology productively. Make sure you book your school's devices in advance, and always do personal trial runs of the activity before you do it with your class.

- Be careful, but enthusiastic when using smart phone and tablet cameras. Make sure that your learners are only using cameras for the intended activity, and are not taking pictures of each other and then sharing the photographs on social media! Use tablet and smart phone cameras to:

    o Scan codes

    o Make animations

    o Make movies

    o Make memes and magazine covers

    o Take photographs of homework tasks

    o For any other task that you (or the students) can think of

- Make use of a wide range of online activities involving smart phones, tablets and mobile technology including:

    o Scheduling homework through various calendars

    o Producing graphs for project-based work

    o Turning the device into a 'clicker' for quizzes

- o Voice-commanded research

- o Watching educational videos

- o Peer assessment by sending each student another person's work and enabling them to submit detailed and focused feedback through a Google™ form (or similar)

- Book your school's ICT labs if they happen to be free when you are teaching. Plan these lessons thoroughly, so that maximum productivity is achieved.

- Use social media to get your students to effectively share content, collaborate and carry out research. Make sure your students are of the required age to use the platform, and make sure they follow the S.M.A.R.T. acronym.

- Train your students to be independent learners by forcing them to come up with the technological solutions to the problems/tasks that you set them. The demand for problem-solving skills in the corporate workforce has never been higher and that trend is set to continue long into the future. Students need to know how to teach themselves to use new ICT systems that they are unfamiliar with – it's the best preparation they can get for the 'real world'.

CHAPTER 6

Working With Parents: Learn to make your key customers happy!

"A genuine commitment to work co-operatively with parents should be a feature of any high-quality setting and should impact on every aspect of practice."

Jane Drake (Author of Learning in the Foundation Stage)

T he key to any successful business relationship is making your customers feel happy. The computer games manufacturer needs to make software that's user-friendly, desirable and value for money. The restaurant owner needs to offer tasty and nutritious food in a good location, served with a smile and at the right price. An online dating agency needs to provide a range of desirable candidates, ease of interface and attractive promotions. The list goes on and on. For a teacher, excellent lesson delivery, good communication with home, excellent feedback to students and a willingness to listen are all essential components of your key business relationship: the one between you and the parents of your students.

In this chapter, we'll be examining the parent-teacher relationship in detail, with the hope of discovering ways in which to satisfy our key customers. A good place to start is the 'Seven Key Desires of Parents'.

The Seven Key Desires of Parents

Parents want teachers to:

1. Be easily reachable, and to reply to them quickly when they raise an issue or have a question

2. Listen attentively to any concerns, issues or queries they may have

3. Deal with any concerns they have, quickly!

4. Uphold professional standards, and be role models for their children

5. Assign grades fairly, based on good assessment practice

6. Inform them immediately if their children are underperforming in any way

7. Be understanding and sympathetic towards any special educational needs or language barriers present (e.g. if a child's native language is not English), or any other extenuating circumstances

As we progress through this chapter, we shall be examining the secrets that make all effective teachers satisfy these seven desires. If you get this right, your parents will be happy and they will praise you in front of their friends, children, other parents and even the senior managers at your school. If you get this wrong, then you can expect the complete opposite to happen!

Secret number 29: Treat parent consultations as if they were job interviews

Parents who have the time to spare and who care deeply about their child's education usually come along to parents' 'evenings' or 'consultations'. It is a great opportunity for you to build good relationships with these key individuals, and to find out new information about your students. A parent usually wants the following from a parent-teacher meeting:

1. To feel welcomed and valued

2. The teacher to listen carefully to what he or she is saying (without interrupting)

3. The teacher to show that he or she genuinely cares about the success of the child

4. Lots of useful, easy-to-understand, accurate data about the student (it's great if you can actually give a copy of this to the parent)

5. To receive good advice and to have his or her questions answered accurately

The teacher should treat any meeting with a parent just like a job interview. This means that you need to do the following:

- Be punctual to the meeting (ideally you should be sat at your desk before the parents arrive)

- Dress appropriately

- Smell good: This may sound patronising, but parents always remember a teacher who smells bad. Remember: you're supposed to be a role model, right? Make sure you've deodorised and taken a breath mint before the consultation begins. If your parent-teacher meeting is immediately after a busy day at work, it is easy to forget to do this. First impressions count, so make sure that yours is a good one.

- Look fresh: Make sure you've had a good sleep the night before, and make sure you've prepared all of the documents and data you will need for the meeting **well in advance** (the day before at the latest)

- Prepare all of your student records well. If you have time, then prepare individual copies for parents. Remember to rehearse in your mind what you will say about each student. Never leave a parent-teacher meeting to chance; you can't afford to be ad-hoc in your approach.

- Speak clearly. This is especially true if the parent you are speaking with is not a native English speaker. Try not to mumble, and don't talk too fast.

Let's now look at some exemplar dialogues. As an activity, I'd like you to try and identify the good and bad points of each of them.

Dialogue 1: Mr. Price and Emily's Mother

(Parent approaches the teacher's desk)

Mr. Price: (Remains seated) "Hi. Please sit down."

Parent: "Hi. I'm Emily's mother. How's my daughter doing in class?"

Mr. Price: "Which year group is Emily in?"

Parent: "Year 10"

Mr. Price: "Ah yes! I remember her. Generally she is doing really well. She is always polite and punctual, she hands in work on time and she presents her class work really well. She can be a bit chatty at times though."

Parent: "Oh, okay. That sounds positive, generally. How are her grades?"

Mr. Price: "Pretty good. I don't have her data with me at the moment. However, I can call or e-mail you tomorrow with more information, if you like?"

Parent: "Right. I see. Yes, please do e-mail me tomorrow. Do you have my e-mail address?"

Mr. Price: "Yes, I have access to it via our school's database"

Parent: "Okay. That's great. So do you have any recommendations or advice that I can pass on to Emily?"

Mr. Price: "Just tell her to keep up the good work. Nothing really stands out as being a cause for concern"

Parent: "Okay. Thank you for your time. See you soon"

Mr. Price: "Thank you. See you soon"

(The parent stands up and leaves. The teacher remains seated and does not shake her hand or acknowledge her departure in an appropriate way)

Activity

Now that you have read through this conversation between Mr. Price and Emily's mother, write down your thoughts on the following:

- What did Mr. Price do well?

- What could Mr. Price have improved upon?

Try to think about both the verbal and non-verbal elements of this parent-teacher interaction. A reflection follows.

Dialogue 1: Reflection

Whilst this parent-teacher interaction was probably a lot shorter than one would expect in reality, it does demonstrate some particularly poor teacher behaviours that are, unfortunately, common to many dialogues at parents' evening. These are listed below:

1. Mr. Price should have stood up, greeted the parent with a smile and a handshake (or whatever the customary greeting would be in his culture or locality) and invited the parent to sit down.

2. Throughout this consultation, Mr. Price bases his feedback on vague memories and intuition. In fact, one could be forgiven for thinking that Mr. Price could be making up a lot of his vague descriptions because he has nothing concrete to offer. What the parent of this middle-school child really needs is good, reliable data about Emily so that she can scrutinise it in more detail and act upon it if necessary. Mr. Price's contributions to this dialogue would seem like a quick way to please the parent in the vaguest way possible. He's telling her what he thinks she would want to hear. Could it be that Mr. Price has forgotten who Emily is? Did Mr. Price look over Emily's data before the consultation? Is Mr. Price on the defensive, trying to make this parent pleased for the time being?

3. When asked for any recommendations or advice, Mr. Price simply responds with a "keep up the good work". This kind of statement, whilst it is positive and encouraging, isn't really detailed enough. Even for the most determined and intelligent students, there should always be at least one item of specific, constructive feedback that the teacher can offer. Could Mr. Price have recommended a specific book or piece of equipment for the parent to purchase? Perhaps a good website for the Emily to look at? Could he have mentioned a specific revision method that would help prior to tests or exams? Is Emily easily distracted in class (as Mr. Price alluded to)? If so, then how could he work with the parent to solve this?

4. Mr. Price was not sure which year group Emily was in. This could indicate that he has not forged a particularly strong professional relationship with that student. If Mr. Price taught two or more students by the name of 'Emily', then he should have clarified which child it was in a more specific way, such as "Would that be Emily in Year 10 or Year 12?" or "Emily Smith or Emily Jones?"

5. At the end of the conversation, Mr. Price should have summarised the main conclusions and action points of the meeting and asked the parent if she was happy with the quality of feedback received (remember: parents are your key customers).

6. The conversation seemed quite 'robotic' and inhuman in nature. Was Mr. Price trying to get this dialogue over with as quickly as possible?

7. The one main positive feature was that Mr. Price does agree to follow up with the parent by e-mail. This is a good strategy, and you should always agree to get back to a parent if you can't answer a query at that instant. However, you must NEVER just give lip-service to this. You must always actually do the following-up, if you've agreed to do so with the parent.

You may be able to think of other positives and negatives for this conversation. How would you have dealt with Emily's mother differently? Could you tell which subject specialism Mr. Price taught from the conversation he had with her? In the next example, we'll see a very different type of interaction take place.

Dialogue 2: Mrs. Jones and Mr. Maxwell

(The parent approaches the teacher's desk. Mrs. Jones stands up, smiles and makes eye contact with the parent)

Mr. Maxwell: "Hi"

Mrs. Jones: "Hi. Lovely to see you. I'm Mrs. Jones. Please take a seat"

Mr. Maxwell: "Thank you"

Mrs. Jones: "How can I help you today?"

Mr. Maxwell: "My son is Lewis Maxwell in Year 7. How's he getting on?"

Mrs. Jones: "Ah! Fantastic! It is an honour to meet the parent of such a talented student! Lewis has produced a lot of detailed, high quality class work this half-term, in which his scientific diagrams are particularly detailed. He always hands in his homework on time, and it is usually of a very high standard".

Mr. Maxwell: "Wow. That's so good to hear. He does put a lot of time into his homework actually"

Mrs. Jones: "Yes, I agree. I've certainly spotted that. I think that we can safely say that Lewis is a young man who has a very good work-ethic. Would you agree?"

Mr. Maxwell: (Smiles and laughs). "Yes, I guess so. But then again, I am biased"

Mrs. Jones: (Laughs). "I think we're all permitted to be a little biased when it comes to our own kids. I think now would be a good time for me to show you some of Lewis' data and his work, so that I can really show you the specifics of how good he is. Would that be okay?"

Mr. Maxwell: "Yes. That sounds great."

(Mrs. Jones now goes through her records and uses the data to verify the claims she made earlier in the conversation. Assessment scores, homework grades and class work data are all looked at, along with some examples of Lewis' class notes.)

Mrs. Jones: "Now that we've looked at the many positives about Lewis and his work, I think we should look at targets for the future. We're a team, me and you, Mr. Maxwell, and I'd very much like to work with you to help Lewis with something. Are you happy with that?"

Mr. Maxwell: "Yes, of course. I totally agree. I'm willing to do anything I can to help"

Mrs. Jones: "Well, I'm certainly very pleased to hear that, because, let me assure you, not every parent is as open to constructive feedback as you are!" (Mrs. Jones smiles). "Lewis does tend to get confused when using key vocabulary. He often writes the wrong word for a process or label on a diagram. However, I think we can solve this if we agree to allow Lewis to learn three new words and their meanings each lesson".

Mr. Maxwell: "That sounds like a good plan, and I'm glad you've picked up on this actually. Only last week he was describing the greenhouse effect to me and he mentioned something like 'nitrogen gas' when he should have been talking about carbon dioxide".

(They both exchange a giggle)

Mrs. Jones: "Okay then. So what I shall do for Maxwell is that I shall ask him to highlight three key words per lesson, and write the definitions for them in his science book. Would you be okay to help me with this by going through this task with him on the day it's given?"

Mr. Maxwell: "Well, I check his planner every day anyway, just to make sure I know what work he has, but yeah, definitely, I'll look at those key words with him. If I can't because I'm busy then I'll ask his mother to step in and do that"

Mrs. Jones: "Brilliant! That's such a big help and I really appreciate it. Well, I think we've covered everything, unless I've missed something?"

Mr. Maxwell: "No, I think that's everything. Thank you for your time. I'm pleased that Lewis is doing so well"

Mrs. Jones: "It's my pleasure, Mr. Maxwell. I'll start the vocabulary reinforcement next lesson, which will be tomorrow. If you ever have any questions or concerns between now and the next time we meet, then please do let me know"

(Mrs. Jones and Mr. Maxwell stand up, shake hands and smile)

Mr. Maxwell: "Likewise. Thanks once again. See you next time"

Mrs. Jones: "See you next time. Enjoy the rest of the evening"

Okay. Clearly this was a very different kind of dialogue than the conversation between Mr. Price and Emily's mother. See if you can answer the questions in the next activity.

Activity

Having now read through dialogue 2, answer the following questions:

- How was this conversation different to dialogue one?

- How did Mrs. Jones make the parent feel welcome and important?

- Which strategies did Mrs. Jones use to tell the parent about her concerns regarding Lewis?

- Do you think that Mrs. Jones prepared for this meeting in advance? If so, then what kind of preparations did she make?

- What could Mrs. Jones have done better?

As soon as you have thought about these questions, please read through the reflection.

Dialogue 2: Reflection

This conversation was very different to dialogue one for a number of different reasons:

- Mrs. Jones greets the parent with a smile and makes him feel welcome. She says that it's "lovely to see you" in a sincere tone of voice. The effect of this simple gesture of acknowledgement is absolutely magical, and Mr. Maxwell now feels respected and is acknowledged as being an important person: a parent. The is the first thing you should always do when meeting with a parent, and it has the added benefit of being a 'temper diffuser' too (in that it helps to put a parent in a positive frame of mind: especially important if he or she has come into school with a number of complaints or concerns in mind).

- Throughout this conversation, the parent is made to feel valued and appreciated. Mrs. Jones talks about forming a "team" with Mr. Maxwell and she commends him for being "open to constructive feedback" (and, crucially, **she means it**).

- Mrs. Jones clearly had a point of concern on her mind: she had noticed that Lewis was not using subject-specific vocabulary correctly. Had she have just blurted this out towards the start of the conversation, then Mr. Maxwell may have immediately decided to go on the defensive and become confrontational. Nobody in this world enjoys being criticised. Additionally, anything associated with the word 'my' is automatically placed under close identity protection by the human mind. This includes concepts such as 'my style', 'my taste in music', 'my accent' and even – you guessed it – 'my son' and 'my daughter'. To avoid challenging Mr. Maxwell's perception of Lewis (and Mr. Maxwell's own dignity and identity along with it), Mrs. Jones raised her concern in a very intelligent and tactful way:

    1. She spent the majority of the first part of the conversation getting Mr. Maxwell to agree with her, and to say a very uplifting and psychologically powerful word: _yes_. Mr. Maxwell says the word 'yes' three times in this conversation (and probably a few more times as he was looking at Lewis' data) prior to being informed about the vocabulary issue. This is a very simple application of what psychologists call the 'Socratic Method', so named after the great Socrates: a Greek philosopher who advocated the practice of finding 'common ground' with a person first, before presenting a statement or argument that may otherwise have been rejected by the listener[8].

---

[8] Carnegie, D. (1981). *How to win friends and influence people.* New York: Pocket Books.

This is an incredibly powerful tool to use when dealing with any human interaction, not just ones between you and the parents of your students. By agreeing with what Mrs. Jones was saying, Mr. Maxwell was being physiologically ***primed*** for the suggestion that his son had an issue with his vocabulary usage. As you can see from the conversation, Mr. Maxwell received this 'criticism' with good grace, and was even open to the idea of working with Mrs. Jones to solve the problem.

2. Mrs. Jones reinforces the parent's sense of importance and value by reminding him that he is a part of the "team". Mrs. Jones wants his help and feedback, and Mr. Maxwell agrees to "check his planner every day" and help with the vocabulary reinforcement.

3. All of Lewis's positive attributes are mentioned first. Mrs. Jones talks about his "high-quality class work" and the detail present in his scientific diagrams. She says that Lewis is a student "who has a very good work-ethic", and this makes Mr. Maxwell feel proud and happy. Again, crucially, she means what she says, and this primes the parent well for any improvement targets she wishes to raise later on.

- Did you notice that this conversation was very human in nature? It has a nice 'chatty', relaxed feel to it. It is not a robotic exchange of information, but is a friendly and professional liaison between two people who are working together for a common purpose: to help the student to succeed.

- Mrs. Jones commits to taking action, stating that she will "start the vocabulary reinforcement next lesson". This provides a positive outcome of the meeting with the parent, rather like a doctor prescribing suitable medication after an initial consultation.

- Mrs. Jones makes sure that the parent is happy to finish the conversation, before saying her goodbyes. She asks if there's anything she's missed, offering a lead into the farewell exchange.

- As a point for improvement, perhaps Mrs. Jones could have summarized the main points of the meeting at the end of the conversation. Mentioning a brief overview of all of Lewis's positives and his targets for the future would have helped Mr. Maxwell to remember them more solidly. However, when one is pushed for time (as is often the case in parent consultations), it can be difficult to get this part done.

Parent consultations summary

- Always welcome your parents with a smile and an appropriate greeting

- Begin the consultation with the things you agree upon

- Get the parent saying 'yes' immediately

- Make the parent feel valued. Thank them for their time and effort with your student.

- Always go through the positive attributes of your student, before introducing the negatives as 'targets for improvement'

- Always have accurate data prepared. This allows you to back-up your statements and talk about positives and negatives in terms of assessment grades.

- Talk in terms of a 'team-mentality'. Make the parent feel involved by talking about how you can work together to help the student.

- Mention any action items that you can implement. Make sure you act on them!

- Be sincere! Make sure you mean what you say.

- Summarize the discussion at the end, if time allows

- Always show that you are available at any time if the parent has any future questions or concerns. Once again, this falls into the 'customer satisfaction' category. Treat your parents as if they are your valued customers, and they will love you for it!

Secret number 30: Learn to be a good listener

"One of the most sincere forms of respect is actually listening to what another has to say."

Bryant H. McGill (American author, aphorist, speaker and activist)

The overwhelming majority of parents want their children to succeed in life. In most cases, hard-working students will become successful people and go on to further study or climb their way up the business ladder. For some students, however, immense amounts of hard-work are not enough to overcome personal barriers such as poor language proficiency, Special Educational Needs or even domestic issues beyond their control. However, no matter what the circumstances are surrounding the life of the child, parents will expect teachers to deliver results. So, how do we satisfy parents when enough is never enough?

In truth, no matter how great a teacher you are there will always be parents who are dissatisfied with something. In many cases these parents do have legitimate concerns, and the first and most effective way to begin tackling these issues is to listen, *carefully!* This may seem like an obvious and simple point to make, but how many people actually know *how* to listen? Have you ever spoken at length to someone who was fiddling with their smart phone instead of making eye contact with you? How did that feel? Did you ever explain something to someone who seemed as though they were listening, only to then ask them a question and be met with confusion? "Sorry, what did you just say, darling?" Have you ever been rudely interrupted mid-conversation before getting your main point across? How did you respond to that?

Business leaders, sales executives, psychologists and counselors understand the power of good listening skills. When a person is allowed to talk at length, the following happens:

- The person feels valued and important

- Heightened emotions diffuse away as the person 'gets something off their chest'

- A feeling of reassurance is induced

- A friendly connection builds between the speaker and the listener

I remember taking a long flight from London to Abu Dhabi (and then on to Bangkok) as I relocated to start my first international teaching post. A very friendly Thai lady was sat next to me on the plane as she was going home to see her family and friends for the first time in four years. For the entire flight she told me all about her family members, her employment history, funny stories about her time in the UK and she even taught me some Thai phrases. I listened attentively, and I laughed and smiled with her as she recalled awkward situations when she couldn't speak English properly and was misunderstood, and when she had to find unusual ways to improvise as she cooked Thai food using British ingredients. At the end of the flight, when it was time for us to say our goodbyes, she said something which I've never forgotten: "You know, Richard, you're the most interesting person I've ever met". Interesting? Wow! How could that be? I hadn't spoken about myself at all during that flight; all I had done was listen to her!

Quick tips on being an effective listener

1. Allow the other person to talk at length. Do not interrupt unless you have to (e.g. if you have an important phone call to take or if you have something urgent to attend to).

2. Ask the person good questions at appropriate times during the conversation. The two types of questions which are most effective are those that *summarise,* and those that *further the conversation.* For example:

   a. "Right, Mr. Butler. I think I understand. So what you're saying is that Andrew is not coping with his current workload, and needs extra time to complete assignments.

Is that correct?" – This would be a summation question (this had the added effect of *reassuring* the parent that you've been listening in the first place).

    b.   "That's fantastic. The work you've done with Sarah has certainly helped her to slow down her writing in class. How do you find the homework I'm giving her? What are your thoughts about how hard it is?" – This question furthers the conversation, and can be a good way to get a 'waffling' parent back on track and focussed on the points you wish to raise.

    c.   "Okay. Correct me if I'm wrong Mrs. Doherty, but what you're mostly concerned about is the teasing she is being subject to in class? Would that be a fair comment?" – Again, this is a question that aims to summarise and reassure.

3.   Your whole physiology must match that of a person who is interested in the person doing the talking. Look at the person when they talk, smile, nod your head when you agree with something and make sure you spot (and respond to) any questions raised.

4.   Encourage the other person to continue talking with subtle hints such 'yes' and 'uh huh'.

Secret number 31: Use detached objectivity

Have you ever had someone come up to you and blatantly tell you off? Have you ever dealt with someone who was confrontational or aggressive, and who was looking for an argument? Perhaps it was a student, a parent or a colleague. How did it make you feel? What was your gut reaction?

When most people are faced with a situation like this, their instinct is to have an *emotional* response. You may feel like you want to justify yourself, or that you're being treated unfairly. When this happens we often fall into the trap of arguing back and 'telling the other person a thing or two'. As soon as it's all over though, tempers settle down and regret may take root: "Oh no, I was so silly. I shouldn't have let myself get angry".

Jonathan was a new Year 5 primary school teacher with responsibility for 24 students. Most of his pupils were cheerful and compliant, causing few problems. However, one child in particular always used to 'play up' and 'act like a clown'. This young boy, David, was notorious for getting 'over-excited': singing songs when he should have been listening, making silly noises and getting into fights. He had a bad reputation, and unfortunately this affected Jonathan's perception of him as a student of worth. Students in the class would tease him (as they had done for years), and this would cause David to respond like most kids would; by being emotional. What Jonathan didn't know was that David had quite an unhappy life at home, often being neglected and being left to fend for himself. No wonder David was seeking attention at school: he certainly didn't receive much at home. To make matters worse, his mother was notorious for being argumentative and 'rough'.

Parent consultations came up towards the end of the first semester. David's mum was present, and she had a thing-or-two to say to Jonathan! Sitting at Jonathan's desk she got straight to the point:

"You're the worst teacher David has ever had. He gets bullied in your class by everyone and his books haven't been marked in two weeks! It's not acceptable. What are you going to do about it? Go on, tell me!" This caught Jonathan by surprise and he could feel the anger boiling up inside himself. He had to let it out. He had to tell this woman what he thought about David, and her too!

"What am I going to do about it? What am I going to do about it? Let me tell you something! David is a silly little kid who has no manners, completes scruffy and atrocious work and who needs to learn how to tie his shoelaces properly before he can understand anything remotely complex, like mathematics or English. He's the only kid in my class who causes problems. No wonder the other kids tease him: he's an absolute lunatic. I have to wonder: what the hell is going on at home? You haven't really done your job as a mother very well at all, have you?" Jonathan felt good now that he had gotten this off his chest, but not for long. An argument soon ensued, with voices getting louder and louder. People's heads started turning to see the commotion, and everyone knew straight away – *that's David's mum.*

Did Jonathan deal with this parent well? Was this mother treated with the respect she deserved, being a key customer of this school? David's mother asked to see the headmistress, and after being ushered into her office she broke down in tears. She complained about being a single mother trying to look after three kids and hold down two jobs at the same time. She laid it all out and explained the problems she had at home, and how she couldn't always look after David as best as she'd like. She talked about her financial problems, health problems, difficulties with David's father and anything else that came to mind. In short, she told a very sad story which certainly tugged at the heartstrings. Who do you think the headmistress was angry with at the end this discussion? Was she ready to remove David from the school? Was she hoping to wash her hands of this crying, sad mother who had just confided in her? No. She was angry at one person only: Jonathan.

Jonathan had made a crucial mistake with this parent: a mistake that gets repeated across the world every day and which spans a range of professions and human interactions. Jonathan had chosen to respond *emotionally* to this parent's verbal onslaught, instead of responding *rationally*. If Jonathan had used the tried-and-tested technique of detached objectivity, then this whole charade would have ended in a much nicer way.

What is detached objectivity?

Detached objectivity is a way of visualizing a situation as being removed (or detached) from yourself, and then working with the other party to come up with a range of possible solutions to the problem. It requires self-control and good listening skills, and an ability to remove your emotions from an unfolding issue. This method nearly always leads to the person doing the complaining to calm down, and it is a good way to diffuse an argument before it explodes like a time-bomb!

"If you don't want to be in an argument with someone, it is probably best to try to solve the problem, rather than lying around hoping the other person will do it for you."

Emily Lockhart (Author of We Were Liars)

Jonathan should have taken Emily's advice and tried to look for a solution, instead of arguing back. A suitable response to the mother's initial critique could have been something like "I certainly agree with you, in that David shouldn't be teased in class, and it is something I've definitely noticed. I'd really like to work with you to come up with some solutions to the issues you've raised. Would that be okay?" From this point onwards, Jonathan could have 'parried' any more character assassinations by remaining calm, listening carefully, staying emotionally detached from the situation and focusing solely on solutions. In fact, it sounds a little bit like being a marriage-guidance counselor (and in some ways, it is).

Secret number 32: Keep parents informed!

This one little secret could save you a lot of hassle and problems as your progress through the academic year. The vast majority of parents appreciate regular communication between home and school: it keeps them up to date and secure in the knowledge that 'all is well'. No parent wants to attend a meeting with a teacher and be suddenly confronted with a big issue concerning their child, if they haven't been informed about the issue in advance. If a parent has not had the opportunity to deal with their child's problem (e.g. persistent lateness to class) in their own way, then it is unfair to suddenly drop it on their lap like a lead weight! Additionally, failure to keep your parents fully informed along the way is like adding petroleum to a pile of wood before you set it alight: it's likely to result in dissatisfaction and, possibly, a confrontation.

Most schools now offer a variety of methods by which you can communicate with parents. What follows next is a list of top tips to help you keep your parents: your key customers, updated with anything that's going on in class.

Keeping your parents informed – top tips

Remember: All communication with parents must be professional in tone and concise. Always remember to inform key individuals too (e.g. you may need to inform the child's homeroom teacher or 'form tutor', your head of department, other subject teachers or even your head of school). You need to gauge the type of communication that's appropriate to the situation at hand.

- *E-mail*: Many schools will have a parent's database that you can access. If not, then get the relevant e-mail address from your school office. Remember to cc' relevant individuals, and if you don't get a reply then you may need to follow up using a different communication tool.

- *Telephone*: Telephone conversations are usually more effective at building rapport between you and the parent than e-mail is. E-mail lacks the emotional overtones and voice inflections that come with a phone call. Make sure you pick your time to call wisely (remember: in many families both parents work during the day), and don't forget to keep a written record of your conversation.

- *Virtual Learning Environments (VLE's)*: These come in many different forms but often include interactive web pages, blogs, homework databases and messaging functions built in. Make sure that parent permissions are enabled for your school's VLE, and keep your pages updated!

- **Written notes**: A quick and easy way to send a message home. Notes can be written inside student planners, notebooks, on loose paper or even in a special 'contact book'. Make sure you have some way of verifying that the notes have been seen by the parent though! You may wish to ask the parent to sign or respond to a written note that's given to a student, or you may wish to follow up with a phone call or an e-mail.

- **Social media**: This is fast becoming a novel and cheap way for schools to communicate with parents. Platforms such as Facebook™, Instagram™ and Twitter™ offer page setup for free, with quick connectivity features. Whilst this is good for whole school announcements and big event updates, it isn't really appropriate for contacting parents with specific issues unless private messaging functions are enabled. ***Never connect with a parent or student through your personal social media profile.***

Secret number 33: Deal with all issues quickly!

Have you ever had someone promise you that they would do something, only to then forget or just simply not commit to the action they said they would take? If you've paid for your car to be washed only to find it dirtier than ever upon your return, how would you react to that? As teachers, we unwittingly make these mistakes on a regular basis. We're always so busy: marking books, planning lessons, attending meetings, teaching classes, preparing resources and so on. Under these circumstances, it is easy to forget to e-mail that parent like you said you would last week, or begin those lunchtime revision sessions that you agreed to host when you spoke with your math students yesterday.

As teachers, we need to be *super organized*, especially when it comes to working with parents. Remember to note everything down in your planner, and take action when you said you would. When a parent e-mails or messages you in any way, make sure you respond quickly (no more that 24 hrs is appropriate). If you can't effectively deal with the issue being sed in 24 hours, then at least send a message back to the parent as an acknowledgment and to let them know that you're 'onto it'. The parents will thank you for it, and the effect on the learning of your students will multiply as they realize that you are 'on the ball', and that they can't get away with anything. Also, don't forget that parents talk to their children at home, so you want them to sing your praises, not criticize you.

Working With Parents: Summary

- Treat parent consultations as if they are job interviews. This means that you should be well-prepared, punctual and you should give the best impression of yourself, the school and the student as you can. Always emphasise the strong points of a student before discussing any areas for improvement, and make a note of any special requests that your parents have (e.g. vocabulary lists or extra homework).

- Be a good listener. Remember to never interrupt, always repeat back what the parent has told you and speak in terms of working 'as a team'. Try your best to resolve any reasonable concerns that parents have. Sometimes parents just want to "get something off their chest' and want to know that they've been heard. Be receptive, even if you're being personally criticised, and work with parents to find solutions to any issues that arise.

- Always discuss a plan of action, and resolve to do what you've promised

- Keep your parents informed about their children along the way, especially if any issues arise. No parent wants to be surprised with bad news at a parent-teacher conference or an end of year report.

- There is no such thing as an 'off-duty' teacher. You're expected to be a role-model at all times, especially when dealing with parents. Societies around the world, in general, hold teachers in high regard. For this reason, we are duty bound to live-up to that ideal by speaking politely, dressing neatly and conducting ourselves with decorum, reserve and grace in all of our interactions on a daily basis.

- Use detached objectivity when dealing with 'difficult' or 'confrontational' parents. Remember: Listen carefully, remove your emotions from the situation and try to think of sensible solutions to the problem.

- Respond to parents quickly and efficiently, no matter what medium they've used to contact you. If the issue is complex and needs time on your part (e.g. Writing a reference letter), then at least acknowledge that you've received the message and that you'll do your best to address the request as soon as possible.

CHAPTER 7

Working With Colleagues: Creating and maintaining professional relationships

"Every successful individual knows that his or her achievement depends on a community of persons working together."

Paul Davis Ryan (Chairman of the U.S. House Budget Committee)

Teachers are generally very well-educated. We've been all the way through different school systems as children and adolescents, and many of us have an array of impressive university qualifications. When one also considers our varied and extensive experience, along with the continuing professional development that we're all subject too, it's realistic and accurate to make the conclusion that teachers are among the most esteemed professionals on the planet. I bet you feel good now, don't you?

It's true. We should be proud of ourselves. However, sticking a bunch of intelligent, opinionated (let's be honest with ourselves) and experienced people together in a professional setting can sometimes be a recipe for a big headache! I've met them all during my ten years as a secondary teacher and tutor. I've had the pleasure of working with extremely helpful and understanding colleagues both in the UK and internationally, and I've also had the challenge of working with some, let's say, 'interesting' people. Rumormongers, backstabbers, gossipers and drama queens and kings; if you haven't come across these personalities in your career thus far, then don't become complacent, because you're bound to meet them sooner or later.

This chapter aims to outline the behaviours and the mindsets that you should adopt if you wish to work productively with your colleagues. You'll also identify the key behaviours to avoid, and the situations that can create them. You'll learn how to resolve conflicts, and how to make your colleagues like you and enjoy working with you.

Secret number 34: Your colleagues are not your friends

Wow! There's a shocker right off the bat, but it's true. Whilst professional relationships can mature into wonderful 'friendships', you must always remember that that your colleagues are the people you work with. That means that they are always capable of reporting you to senior management behind your back, whilst pretending to be nice to your face.

They can undermine your work practices if they wish, and they can even stop you from getting that key promotion, if they feel it will benefit them in the short or long-term.

Sharon was an incredibly intelligent and enthusiastic English teacher, who had just relocated from Los Angeles to Chicago, as her husband had to transfer to a new office. She had enjoyed working at her previous all-girls school, where she regularly went out for drinks with her colleagues and enjoyed a cosy, relaxed and friendly school atmosphere.

Upon arriving at her new school, Sharon was keen to get to know everyone and make friends with her new workmates. She attended the school's welcome meal and drinks for new staff, and she started to socialise with the other girls at work. She became very close to one colleague in particular: Clarissa, and they would both go out to play squash and badminton together and they lived very close to one another. They we're always in each other's apartments, and enjoyed sharing stories and gossip about other people at work.

As the first semester break approached, Sharon was quite behind on her marking. The business of relocating to a new city, along with the adjustment to a new school's set of systems and procedures had eaten up a lot of her time. She invited Clarissa over to her place one evening that week for drinks and a chat. They both had a nice evening, and they talked for hours. During the conversation, Clarissa mentioned her backlog of marking, only as a 'passing comment'.

What Sharon didn't know was that Clarissa was also very good friends with Michael: the head of the English department and a member of the Senior Leadership Team. Clarissa had been going out with Michael and a group of friends to attend a pub quiz every week for about two years. I'm sure you can guess what happened at the next outing she had with Michael: at one point in the evening she told him about Sharon and how she was struggling to complete all of her marking, again, as a 'passing comment'.

Why did Clarissa tell Michael about Sharon's problem? Perhaps it came up in friendly conversation. Maybe Clarissa wanted to make herself look good. Was Clarissa concerned about Sharon, and wanted to let her line manager know so that he could support her? Who knows? What is certain though is that it doesn't really matter what the reason was. The information was passed on, and now Sharon would have to deal with the aftermath.

When Michael came into school the following Monday, one of the first things he did was look through Sharon's student notebooks. To him, this 'passing comment' made by Clarissa was not something to be overlooked. His school ethos was one of high expectations: both for students and for staff. Additionally, as a member of the Senior Leadership Team, he wasn't about to allow a member of his department make him look bad, and he wasn't prepared to leave the issue and take the risk of having a parent complain at some point in the future. Upon inspecting the books, Michael was concerned when he discovered that they hadn't been marked since the first day of term. He scheduled a meeting with Sharon, and basically told her to get those books marked ASAP, and that he would be checking after the term break had finished.

How do you think Sharon felt after this conversation? That's right: she was not best pleased. She felt betrayed and embarrassed, and the happy atmosphere that she had associated with this new school had now been shattered into a million pieces. She was annoyed with Clarissa for talking about her 'behind her back', especially when she felt that she had spoken with her friend 'in-confidence' (oh, how often we misjudge that one!). She learnt the hard way the lesson that some teachers never learn: that your colleagues are not the same as your friends. Needless to say, Sharon and Clarissa's 'friendship' soured after this point, and Sharon (rightly) became far more cautious about what she said in front of her colleagues.

The interesting thing about Sharon's story is that nobody was really in the wrong here. Sharon probably had lots of good reasons for being slightly behind with her marking, and she would soon have gotten her affairs in order without having that chat with Michael. Clarissa, also, may have had sound justification for reporting Sharon's backlog to Michael. She may even have acted out of kindness, being concerned that a parent may complain very soon if those books weren't marked. And Michael, in his role, absolutely had to follow up on what he had heard: he would have been a negligent manager if he hadn't.

Believe it or not, these kinds of stories are very, very common. You may even have experienced something similar to what Sharon went through yourself. Massive amounts of stress and worry are being created in schools all over the world because teachers misinterpret relationships with colleagues. Remember – *your number one job is to keep your job*, and everything you've worked for, **so make sure that your outward actions match the ideal perception that you'd like senior management to have of you.** Never treat your colleagues as if they were your best friends: they're the people you work with, and nothing more.

Secret number 35: The gossip mill produces toxic flour

You and I could walk into any school staff room at morning break time and, after about five minutes, we could easily distinguish between the 'Chatty Cathys' and the 'Reserved Richards'. Gossips love to espouse whatever is on their mind, even if nobody else wants to hear it. They'll tell you one funny anecdote after another, ranging from which salon they went to last week to how difficult they find the new pupil assessment software the school's made them use. There's also one other thing that gossips are really good at, and that's dishing out the dirt on anyone who happens to be the topic of the current conversation.

Gossips, without fail, are people to completely avoid at all costs (where possible). One of the reasons why gossips are famously passed over for promotion is because they can't be trusted with the sensitive information they'd be exposed to in a managerial role. They generate distrust, and you should be very cautious with what you say when around anyone who is a famous gossip; you don't want to give them fuel for a fire that they can burn behind your back! Additionally, if you happen to be sat with a gossip who starts to speak negatively about a colleague or the school in general, then don't be afraid to get up and walk away. *What's more important: having a laugh or having a job?* Besides, do you really want to be sat there when everyone's complaining about the principal and that awkward moment happens when the deputy head walks into the staffroom? If you're sat with gossips, or if you're seen to be hanging around with them and chatting with them frequently, then you'll be associated with them in the minds of senior management. If you plan on having a long and fruitful career in teaching, then remember this golden rule: ***don't gossip, and don't associate with gossips.***

Another point to note is that, if you feel bold enough, you should oppose gossip whenever you hear it (but try not to come over as being bossy or intimidating). If you're planning on entering middle or senior management in your school, then it's in your best interest to shut down the gossip mill before you get promoted; the same people who are gossiping about the leadership style of the Lower Secondary Head will one day be gossiping about you: guaranteed. If you hear gossip that puts anyone in a negative light, then feel free to comment with a "Wow, I would really hate it if someone said something like that about me" or even "I don't think it's right for me to take part in this conversation". Trust me when I say this: gossip is toxic, and you can never be guaranteed anonymity when you spit venom! It's not uncommon for gossip to filter up to management, and if you're name is mentioned when this happens, you may have to endure quite an unpleasant conversation with someone who is rightly annoyed with you.

Secret number 36: Staff parties are not for partying

Now I'm going to tell you the mother of all staff party disaster stories and, unfortunately, I happened to witness the carnage first-hand. I still shudder when I look back and remember the actions of the young man who brought so much agony upon himself. Thankfully, he is okay now and has a good job and two young, healthy children to delight in. Things could have ended up quite differently for him though, and his story offers lots of lessons for us to learn from.

Barry had just been appointed as an English as a Second Language (ESL) teacher at a mixed comprehensive school in the North of England. He was well-qualified, having gained a first class honors degree and a PGCE, and was fresh out of college. Management were excited about having him on board as their first ever ESL specialist, and he was invited to come along to the welcome meal for new staff so that he could meet the new colleagues that he would be working with.

The evening started really well with nice conversation followed by speeches from senior management. Barry and the rest of the 'newbies' were introduced formally, and the party atmosphere kicked in soon afterwards. The school had provided quite a large budget for the event, since they wanted their new staff to really feel valued and welcome. The drink started flowing, with free ale on tap, and the disco lights started to dance around the dimly lit function room. Everyone started to let their hair down, and Barry wasted no time in 'getting into the swing of things'.

Barry had one problem; an issue that had haunted him on many an occasion in his life (and had caused him some problems at university too): he was never able to handle alcohol really well. It made him boisterous, flirtatious, loud and outright aggressive. Tonight was no exception.

He started off pretty normally, enjoying pleasant conversation with his new 'friends'. However, after only one or two drinks, his voice became louder, and he started to get more pushy. He didn't realise how loud he was, but people's heads were starting to turn at every one-liner he shouted, every swear word he spluttered and every laugh he made. If that wasn't enough, he had his eye on a pretty petite blonde-haired lady named Karen, also a new teacher, who was sat a few spaces away from him. When the person who was sat next to her got up to go to the washroom, Barry saw this as his golden opportunity to sit next to Karen and begin 'working his magic'.

Barry was a sophisticated, well-dressed, articulate and handsome young man. He had a series of girlfriends both at high school and at university, and he knew he was attractive. However, he made the almost fatal mistake of thinking that he could treat Karen just like any other girl he'd hooked up with in the past. He was wrong: Karen was his new colleague, and that means a whole new set of rules needs to be followed in, what was to Barry, a very new type of social arena.

Barry slurred his words as he asked Karen her name. He was well-practised in 'pick-ups', and he knew how to get a woman talking. At first he came across as being rather charming, but after a short time the textbook-style, classic flirtations started to roll of his tongue like Thai red curry when you initially thought it wasn't 'that spicy'. "I can tell you are a really sophisticated woman, especially since you dress so well", "What do you look for in a man? I bet you have really high standards, so I guess I must be off your list" and on and on it went, with lots of subtle hints that he was 'interested' in her. A short time later, after enough ale had entered his bloodstream, he felt bold enough to make a pass at her, moving his lips abruptly towards hers. Well that was the guillotine that almost decapitated his career, and what followed next was a chain of events that I'll probably never forget as long as I draw breath.

What Barry didn't know was that Karen had a boyfriend, and he was at this party, sat just opposite from him. Karen and her partner, Adam, had been hired as a 'teaching couple'. Adam had already spotted Barry's obvious advances towards his girlfriend, and after seeing him make this pass, and hearing his girlfriend shout "No" and slap Barry chiefly around the face, Adam flipped out. He got out of his chair and squared up to Barry, and a rather mad brawl ensued between the two men, with all the shouting and kicked over chairs and broken bottles that came with it. The headmaster and the senior managers were dumbstruck, and everyone poured in to split the two men up. The bar manager asked both men to leave, and the whole affair was very embarrassing and cringe-worthy, even for those who were just innocent onlookers like myself.

Had this have been a normal brawl away from the prying eyes of workmates on a Saturday night, then Barry may (and I do mean *may*) have gotten away with this. However, Barry's problems had only just begun, and he had to go to school the following week and start teaching and working with his new colleagues productively. What kind of foundation stones of trust and mutual companionship did Barry lay at that staff party? I think we all know the answer to that: very, very shaky ones!

Immediately after this incident, management had already decided to get rid of Barry as quickly as possible, and that was before he had even met his first students! How could they allow him to spend any great length of time at their school after this outrageous incident? He had planted some rather poisonous seeds of distrust in the minds of his colleagues, and they quickly started to talk about him behind his back. Barry knew what he had done was wrong, and he dreaded going into school for his first day of teaching.

Barry decided to try to make amends as soon as possible, and the first thing he did on his first Monday morning at school (which was an INSET or 'teacher training' day) was to go straight to Karen and Adam and apologise sincerely. They both accepted his apology, but it wasn't enough. His behavior that evening was so bad that all of his colleagues were talking about him behind his back. The headmaster called him into his office for a meeting, and Barry was mortified at the thought of even looking him in the face again. In that meeting, Barry was basically told that his behaviour at the staff party was absolutely atrocious, and that it would take him a long time to gain the trust of his coworkers after this, if he could gain it at all. What Barry didn't know was that, secretly, he had already been set aside for dismissal; management just had to decide which method to use to get rid of him, and how quickly to do it. Sure enough, they removed him at their earliest opportunity, which wasn't very long as Barry had only been signed up on a one year contract.

Surely this is every teacher's worst nightmare, right? You would be surprised at how many teachers, both new and old, let their inhibitions go to ruins when they are socialising with colleagues from school. Barry was lucky this time: the management of his school consisted of sweet 'old-timers' who sympathized (to a limited extent) with Barry as he was a very young man. They provided him with neutral references, and he secured a job at new school before his contract was over. Things could quite easily have gone another way though: the SLT at Barry's school were very generous and understanding in this case, but this is certainly not the status quo for most schools. Tough regulations from local government and accrediting bodies, along with the usual professional ethics requirements that teachers are constantly held subject too, place a lot of pressure on school managers to make sure that they recruit well, and that they root out 'bad apples', quickly. *Make sure that you don't turn into a bad apple through inappropriate behaviour at staff gatherings.*

Secret number 37: Treat e-mails as if they were posters in the principal's office

Sending and receiving e-mails has now become an obligatory duty for secondary school teachers, especially in big institutions. A form tutor asks you for feedback about a particular student, so you e-mail your reply. The deputy head asks for any items for tomorrow's meeting agenda, and those people that have issues they wish to raise type their responses and click 'send'. You have a problem opening a file on a school computer, so you send a quick message to the ICT technician. You e-mail parents. The list goes on and on. As teachers, we are spending more time sat down in front of computers than ever before. E-mails allow us to communicate important items quickly and efficiently, and this 'convenience' is being improved on year after year as 'smart' phones and 'smart' watches increasingly utilise novel systems to make dealing with e-mails an easy and fun task. All of this has made e-mailing become a 'mechanical' part of one's working day, where little thought is needed to deliver a quick message. What most people don't consider, however, is that e-mails are secretly destroying the careers of teachers, along with everything they've worked for.

Charlene was annoyed. She had been slaving away for the past two terms getting her 'A' – Level Chemistry students ready for their final exams. She had lead afterschool revision clubs, printed reams of past-exam papers and resources, spent hours after school planning and setting up practical activities and had spent many a late night updating her school's VLE with a myriad of resources for these senior, pre-university students. She felt that she had gone above and beyond the call of duty, and when Term Three came along and her students were on study leave, she planned to use her gained time to prepare resources for the next academic year.

Knowing that Charlene now had a considerable amount of free time, her head of department, Francis, thought it would be a good idea for her to help the other science teachers alleviate some of their workload. He asked Charlene to take on one of her colleague's Key Stage 3 classes for that term, and he asked Charlene to help assess some of the end-of-year tests for the students in classes that she didn't teach.

Charlene was furious! She felt completely unappreciated and exploited. She had worked her socks off all year, doing things that her other science colleagues didn't have to do, and now she was being asked to do more. She needed to get all of her frustration off her chest, so she decided to e-mail her good friend, Tracey, who happened to be her NQT tutor in her previous school. She laid it all out, saying how her boss was a complete idiot (using some rather colourful language) and how her efforts all year had gone completely unnoticed. She felt really 'hard done to', and typing it all out made her feel much better. However, she made one mistake that proved to be the Armageddon for her career in that school: she sent the e-mail to Francis by accident, and not to her NQT tutor.

This kind of situation happens all the time: teachers sending e-mails to the person they're *talking about*, and not to the intended recipient. For Charlene it was coffin nails for her job at that school. Francis scheduled a meeting with Charlene, and her conclusions were made very clear. She felt that Charlene could have dealt with her frustration in a much more professional way; for example, by simply talking it over with her. If Francis had known Charlene's plans to get some good resources in place for the next academic year, then she would have passed on less work for her to do in her 'gained time'. Additionally, the tone of Charlene's e-mail was so negative and 'immature', that her character as a professional was now being called into question. Could she be trusted as a sensible member of the staff body? What if she had sent an e-mail like that to a parent instead? After Charlene was passed up for promotion the following academic year (because of feedback from her head of department to the school principal), she left by her own accord. To add insult to injury, Charlene's new school needed a reference letter from her current head of department. Thankfully, Francis felt kind enough to emphasise Charlene's good points, as opposed to writing the king of all character assassinations that she could quite easily, and understandably, have produced.

This story teaches us that e-mails should be handled with care. Always take time to craft e-mails properly, and always assume that every person in your school will see it. Never assume e-mail privacy, and always choose your recipients carefully. With the ability to send e-mails through voice-command and touch-screens on smart devices it is even easier to make these fatal mistakes than it ever has been before. Be vigilant!

Think before you send!

- *E-mails are not private*: That's right: you're school principal could be looking through your inbox as you read this! E-mails provide managers with a unique window into an employee's life that they would never normally have in their day-to-day interactions. It is such a good 'teacher monitoring tool' that most schools will now have professional e-mail systems set up for them which allow 'snooping' by senior management. This is perfectly legal, and you've probably signed your consent for it in your employee contract. Many schools are now making all new teachers sign an 'Acceptable use of ICT' agreement, where it will explicitly say that your e-mails should not treated as though they are private. However, despite this, many teachers still do not follow professional e-mail etiquette.

- *Never complain in an e-mail*: There are lots of obvious reasons for this, and many centre around the 'management snooping' issue. Additionally, however, many employees fall into the trap of sending an e-mail to the person they're complaining about, rather than the person it was intended for. This can have apocalyptic consequences for you, especially if the e-mail is sent to a manager. Avoid this by making all e-mails professional, imagining that they'll be blown up to A1 size and posted on the headmaster's wall (because as far as you're concerned, they might as well be).

- *E-mails can be copied, forwarded and saved forever*: Whenever you send an e-mail, you are creating a permanent piece of evidence which may be used against you (or to support you) in the future. E-mailing your best friend to tell them how much time you've wasted drinking coffee today, or how you can't wait for the semester break to come around because you've 'had enough', are not good ways to fill your HR file. I feel it's important to repeat that *you should treat all e-mails as if they were posters in the principal's office.*

- *Extinguish all flames*: A 'flame' is a hostile or insulting message that is sent from one internet user to another. They often contain profanities, expletives or complaints, and in the teaching profession they are most commonly sent and received through e-mail. If you receive a flame from anyone then you must do two things right away:

    1. Respond to the person who sent you the flame, making it clear to them that they should never send you a hostile message via e-mail again. Make it clear that e-mails are not a private messaging tool, and that you do not respond to expletives or profanities. You should also do this for any unprofessional or inappropriate e-mail, such as one from a colleague talking about how much he has slacked off that day.

    2. Delete the original flame e-mail. If your inbox is being monitored, and a member of senior management sees the flame, they may think that you are in agreement with the person who sent it.

Secret Number 38: Don't be a hermit

Inter-colleague relationships require a fine balance between keeping *professional distance*, whilst maintaining a good *social rapport*. With all this talk I've made about how dangerous social gatherings with your workmates can be, along with the toxicity of gossip and e-mails, it can be tempting to think that it's best to shut off all but essential interactions with your fellow coworkers. This is a common but incorrect assumption to make. The teaching profession is strongly people-centred, and requires an atmosphere of mutual trust in order to function normally. If you become a hermit it can become difficult to gain and maintain the trust of your colleagues, since it's difficult to trust someone if you don't know them.

The secret here is really to make sure that you do chat and 'open-up' to your colleagues, ensuring that the impression you make is the best it can possibly be. The following checklist explores the key elements of good coworker interactions.

Open up but not too much: Five tips for maintaining 'Discrete Exposure'

1. *Be a good listener*. High school teachers work with an array of talented and interesting professionals, all of whom are dying to talk about their opinions, experiences and problems. Take the time to sincerely listen to your coworkers, being careful not to interrupt. Repeat elements of the conversation back to the speaker, so as to reassure them that you are listening (e.g. "Oh, so you're keen to do your master's degree in the US" and "I think I understand what you're saying. Basically you suggest that we always write Steven's homework in his planner for him, is that correct?). It was the great Dale Carnegie himself who said *"You can make more friends in two months by being interested in other people than in two years of trying to get people interested in you"*. He was right.

2. *Keep it clean*. Remember, you're talking with your colleagues, not your friends. Avoid crude language, crassness or anything that would be deemed 'inappropriate' for a teacher (even if your colleagues are conversing in this way). A good rule to follow is to treat talking with your coworkers in the same way as if talking with the principal or a parent. This may seem excessive or even patronizing, but you would be surprised at how many 'secret impressions' you make just by the way you talk. It's much better to be overly cautious about what you say and be seen as 'reserved' or 'quiet', than to remove your inhibitions and let everything pour out.

3. *Keep personal information, well, personal*. The music teacher complains about how she can't control her two-year old. The

SENCO is worried about recovery after her next operation, so she blurts out all of her concerns over coffee at break time. The new NQT that the school has just hired says he's stressed about his upcoming wedding preparations, and how they're "eating up" all of his time. What do all of these scenarios have in common? *They give a negative impression of you to your colleagues and to management.* Would you promote someone who had just had a baby and was complaining about how tired she was all the time? Absolutely not! You'd feel as though the extra burden of a higher position would be too much for her. Would you be concerned about the education of your daughter, who happens to be in Year 7 in your school, if her maths teacher was complaining about how he doesn't have the time to prepare his lessons as well as he would like to? Of course you would! The golden rule to remember here is to keep all sensitive and personal information about yourself, to yourself! The only exception to this is when you've done something that puts you in a good light (e.g. telling everyone how happy you are that you've just completed your master's degree).

4. *If you don't agree, then don't agree.* It's all too easy to go along with another person's monologue by unwittingly agreeing with a "Yes, yes", "Indeed" or an "Of course". Be very careful about this, because if you are seen to be agreeing with someone who, for example, is speaking negatively about the school or its management, then you'll also been seen as having the same opinion as that person. This could be the factor that stops you from getting that key promotion, or the issue that makes one of your colleagues just 'shun' you every time you try to talk with him.

5. *Do not reciprocate if it makes you look bad.* Again, it is very easy to do this unwittingly, often as a way to make another person feel better. Managers often use reciprocations as a way to gauge a staff member's competence or performance. For example, if your line manager says "Wow! I don't know about you, but I'm absolutely

snowed-under with marking at the moment", how would you reply? If you respond with a "Yes, I'm in the exactly the same position. I haven't had any time this year to mark my Year 9 books.", then you've just made a classic mistake. The line manager may have been using his friendly approach to find out how you're coping with your workload, and you've just told him! So remember, *keep all reciprocations positive.*

Secret number 39: Don't alienate the 'aliens'

Sometimes it can be overwhelming when you start at a new school, or when a large number of new staff members join your team. It can seem like a major and important challenge when you're trying to make friends with everyone, but it really shouldn't be like that.

Greg was a new psychology teacher at a rapidly growing international school in Brunei. He had come from a school where staff members enjoyed a very close and communal atmosphere: where the men played on football and basketball teams together and the women often played netball, badminton and did aerobics classes. The school was managed well, and staff were encouraged to socialise and be friends with one another. Greg was sorry to leave, but the prospect of more money and a substantially better benefits package tempted him to move on.

Greg's new school was very different to his previous one, but it took him a long time to figure that out. As soon as he started at the school, everyone knew who he was. He would greet everyone loudly and proudly, making jokes and aiming to get everyone laughing in the staff room. He had a lot of opinions about things, from religion to politics and even which teachers in his new school spoke the clearest English, even though he had only been working there for a few weeks. At staff gatherings, including casual chats in the staffroom, he was loud and boisterous and would irritate people with anecdotes and questions, even when they wanted to be left alone. He had an opinion about everything, and he thought that his new colleagues would love him for revealing all of his infallible wisdom and sharing his sense of humour with them. How wrong he was!

Greg made the inconspicuous mistake of alienating his coworkers, to the point where they didn't even want to be around him anymore. He tried to be friends with everyone all at once, and all he ended up doing was irritating people. One member of staff even went so far as to tell him, in front of everyone in the staffroom, "Greg, sometimes I don't know if you're joking or if you're just a complete retard!" This was the statement that woke him up.

Greg eventually toned things down, but it took a while for other staff members to warm to him again. Greg tried to run before he could walk, aiming to make everyone his friend all at once. What he should have done instead is focussed on *making one friend at a time* by taking a sincere interest in his coworkers, and gradually getting to know them.

The old saying 'first impressions count' could not be more applicable to the teaching profession. Schools only function normally when professional trust and shared goals are engrained in the school culture.

Starting your new job (or your interactions with a new group of people) in a high-octane, overpowering way only makes people want to distance themselves from you. Remember: we want our colleagues to be distant enough to respect us as professionals, but we don't want them to be so distant that they don't want to even interact with us.

Secret number 40: Praise and you'll be praised!

A feature that's unique to the teaching profession is that some of the strategies that we use to teach our students effectively, and get them to like us, can also be used to create bonds with our coworkers. The use of sincere praise has long been documented as a key tool in getting our students 'on our side', and this same rule applies to adults too. The great Leo Tolstoy, in his famous novel *War and Peace*, puts it like this:

> *"In the best, the friendliest and simplest relations flattery or praise is necessary, just as grease is necessary to keep wheels turning"*

The next time a colleague of yours leads a workshop or a professional development session, praise them sincerely. Talk about how you really enjoyed the workshop, and how useful it was to you. Be specific: mention things that really stood out for you. Also, don't be afraid to give thanks when someone gives feedback to you, especially if it's negative. Say how much you appreciate the other person taking the time to report this important information to you, and how you'll take what they've said on board. Bosses are particularly important people to praise, since they rarely get acknowledged for their efforts by their team members. The next time the school principal sends you a long e-mail outlining how a new policy will be implemented, or the programme for the next staff training day, praise her! Say how much you appreciated the e-mail because it really clarified things. Be sincere: praise only works if it's genuine.

Secret number 41: Volunteer

Modern secondary school teaching practice is becoming more theme-based and project oriented, with traditional 'rote learning' being replaced with exploration, group work and 'discovery' tasks. As a result, subject teachers increasingly require the assistance of non-specialists for big projects, field trips, events and practical activities.

We're all really busy as secondary teachers, and it can be really tempting to sit back and focus only on your own work when a colleague sends that blanket e-mail around asking for help. Sometimes you will be so busy that you genuinely can't help out, but, where possible, you should offer to lend a helping hand. It's an instant way to get a colleague to like you, and it places you firmly as a 'team player' in the minds of your coworkers and management: a good place to be. Also, with fewer good quality teaching jobs available and with more new graduates entering the profession, competition is high and job security is constantly being compromised. One guaranteed way to make the management of your school want to keep you is to volunteer often (and to do a good job when you do volunteer). They'll love you for it, and they couldn't possibly want to get rid of you. As an added bonus you'll also get to see new dimensions of student and staff life, and this will give you a fresh perspective on your own role within the school: a perspective that can only enhance your effectiveness as an educator.

Working with colleagues: Summary

- Forge friendly, workable relationships with your colleagues, but don't seek consolement too soon (if at all). You need to know a person for a considerable length of time before you can really call him or her a 'friend', and your colleagues should not automatically fall into that category as soon as you get to know them. Be careful what you say or do in front of your colleagues: they work in the same social dynamic as you do, and they can easily report your words or actions to senior management (either covertly or openly).

- Don't gossip, and don't hang around with gossips. If you want to be seen as a trustworthy, dependable member of the staff body, then you need to resist that urge to 'pitch in' when everyone's having a dig at the principal, or something or someone else in the school. Gossips come across as people who cannot keep sensitive information private, and that's exactly the reason why they are commonly passed over for promotion, or worse: fired.

- Be careful about how you behave at staff gatherings and parties. It can be really tempting to let your hair down, especially at the start or end of an academic year, but you must remember that your colleagues and managers are secretly watching you (and judging you) when you're chucking down those pints, shots and bottles of whichever beverage it is that you like. Know your limitations and err on the side of caution: it's much better to come across as being sensible and 'boring' as opposed to 'foolish', 'annoying', 'aggressive' or a 'loud mouth'.

- Treat all e-mails as if they are going to be blown up to size A1 and posted on the principal's notice board. E-mail is not a private messaging tool, and it's very easy to make the mistake of sending an e-mail to the wrong recipient (especially with the advent of mobile technology). Most schools use e-mail systems in which senior managers can easily access you inbox without your permission, if they feel the need to do so. For this reason, keep all of your e-mails professional and work-related. Never complain or use expletives in an e-mail, and remember to extinguish all flames!

- Don't be a hermit, but don't open up too much. Use 'discrete exposure' to form professional relationships with your colleagues, but don't reveal personal information that could be used against you. Remember: teachers are expected to be role models and professionals, and your colleagues will always be secretly judging you, even if they seem like they're your friends.

- Focus on making one 'friend' at a time, as opposed to trying to be best buddies with everyone all at once. If you have a compulsive or energetic personality, then try to tone things down a bit. It can be very easy to alienate the people around you if you're not careful, and you may not even know that you're doing it until someone tells you straight to your face. Try to imagine yourself in the other person's shoes, listening to you drone on and on. Typically, being a good listener works better than being a good talker when forging professional relationships.

- Praise your coworkers and managers in a sincere, genuine way. We all love to feel appreciated and thanked, and your students and colleagues are no different. Sincere praise that has real meaning and comes from the heart is like a magic elixir for mending old conflicts and building new relationships. Insincere flattery, on the other hand, only serves to build distrust and convince people that 'you want something' from them.

CHAPTER 8

Teaching Overseas: Exporting Your Skills to a New Country

"Travel is fatal to prejudice, bigotry, and narrow-mindedness."

Mark Twain

All around me people are chatting, walking, laughing and texting. The smell of spicy glass noodles fills the air, along with the pungent exhaust fumes released from 'tuk-tuks' and motorbikes. Hundreds of these small vehicles rush past every minute as the relentless humidity eats away in the mid-morning sunlight.

I'm at food vendor in old Bangkok, near the sprawling Chinatown district. I've been teaching at international schools in Bangkok for seven years, and I don't miss home one bit. It all started in 2008 when I was teaching in England. One day I went to a friend's house and met a beautiful young Thai girl, who'd just completed her master's degree at Salford University. I fell in love with her, moved to Bangkok with her, and she is now my wife. We've been very happily married for four years. One of the reasons why I decided to include this short addition to the book was so that you could see how well it's worked for me and how classroom management involves added challenges (and rewards) when you decide to teach overseas.

Prior to moving to Thailand I checked out the Times Educational Supplement jobs website (this is where the world's best international schools post their job openings). I found an advertisement for a Science Teacher position at Traill International School in Bangkok and, since this was a CfBT accredited school with an excellent reputation, I applied immediately.

A few weeks later I had an interview with Traill's principal at the Hilton Hotel in Cardiff, Wales. He checked through all of my references, and was impressed enough to offer me the job a few days later. I was thrilled! I was about start a new life in a new country.

My first day of teaching at Traill was a bizarre, but incredibly pleasant experience. I'll always remember the first class I taught: Year 10 IGCSE Chemistry. The students were all so incredibly polite, and were enthusiastic to complete each task I set them. They asked questions, were incredibly interested in the subject and at the end of the lesson every student said "Thank you, Mr Richard" before walking through the door to go to their next class. As I started teaching all of my other classes that week, I found this studious, polite and pleasant student attitude to be ubiquitous. I was stunned! Whilst I had taught many wonderfully polite and enthusiastic students at state schools in the UK, I had never received such a consistent 'whole-school' sense of politeness, eagerness to learn and dedication from my students before. I felt as though I had died and gone to heaven!

Things to do before you teach overseas

- Try to acquire a wide range of teaching experiences. International schools look for candidates who can teach a range of subjects. Whilst being in Bangkok, for example, I have taught general Science, Chemistry, Biology, Mathematics and German to IGCSE level and beyond.

- Look for schools that have been accredited by a professional body, such as the Council for British Teachers (CfBT), the Council of International Schools (CIS) or World Education Services (WES). Schools that are accredited have gone through a rigorous inspection process to ensure that they meet international standards.

- Create a teacher portfolio containing your certificates, examples of marking or assessments and any nice letters, notes or e-mails you've received from parents, students or colleagues. All of these things are golden pieces of evidence that you can present at interview, or even e-mail to the school as part of your application.

- Check your contract before you sign it. Find out if you need a work permit or special visa, and be sure to find out who's supposed to provide this. Check your proposed salary and read carefully through the expected responsibilities for your role.

Advantages of teaching abroad

1. If you choose an accredited school, you'll most likely find that standards are high, student behaviour is excellent and a very generous salary and benefits package awaits you

2. You'll get the chance to experience a new language and culture, which can only serve to enrich your life in many different ways

3. You will gain lots of transferable experiences, such as teaching ESL students and delivering specialist curricula (e.g. The IGCSE and IB Diploma)

4. If you choose your country wisely, your living expenses will be much less than in your native country. Whilst living in Thailand I've bought property, a car and I still have money left over. Back in the UK this would have been nearly impossible for me to do.

5. You'll work with some amazing colleagues, who'll have a wide range of experiences to share with you

6. Most international schools offer an excellent orientation programme, in which you'll get to know your new colleagues (and your new city or town) well

7. Access to services like healthcare will be much more convenient than in your home country, as a good international school will provide you with private health insurance as part of their benefits package. This means that you'll be able to attend private hospitals and be treated on the day, as opposed to the long wait you may endure if restricted by your native country's national health service. Many international schools also have partnerships with hospitals and healthcare providers, so that their teachers feel comfortable and well looked-after.

8. Don't worry if you have a spouse and kids to look after. Most international schools will provide free schooling for your children and, if your partner is a teacher, then they may be able to provide him or her with a job too. Besides, even if your spouse isn't a teacher, he or she can apply for a job at an international company or can even start that business you've been dreaming about for years.

Secret number 42: Teaching overseas is not always easier than teaching at home

Despite the clear advantages listed above, teaching overseas does provide its own unique challenges. If you are seriously planning on relocating to a new country to teach your specialist subject, then you need to consider the following:

Disadvantages of teaching abroad

1. If you can't speak the local language, and you don't have a friend or partner who does, then this can make life difficult. However, a good school will provide full support with this (one of my former colleagues used to bring his Thai mail into school so that the office staff could translate it for him). Also, you should see this as a positive challenge: learning a new language is fun and useful!

2. You'll probably have to teach a far greater number of students who speak English as their second or third language, than you would in your native country. This places extra demands on you in terms of differentiation and making the pace of the lesson match the ability of each student. You may have to speak more clearly and slowly, and you'll probably have to make your lessons as varied and engaging as possible so that maximum learning takes place.

3. The parents of international school students are fee-paying, and therefore they (rightly) have very high expectations. Make sure you employ all of the strategies outlined in the chapter on working with parents, and don't forget that whilst teaching abroad you're not on holiday, and you'll be expected to do an excellent job.

4. Some international schools are very results-driven, and some teachers find the pressure of this to be very overwhelming. However, you should see this as an opportunity to really stretch yourself and gain valuable teaching experience at the same time.

My time in Thailand has been filled with happiness and lots of challenge. I wouldn't change my life one bit, and I never regret leaving the UK all those years ago to teach overseas. It was the best decision I ever made.

Best websites for international teaching jobs and advice

1. *The Times Educational Supplement* (*https://www.tes.co.uk/jobs/*): In my personal opinion, the best international teaching jobs website out there. Schools that post their vacancies on here are usually fully accredited, and you can search for jobs by continent and sign up for e-mail alerts. It's free to sign up, and you can start applying right away.

2. *eTeach International* (*http://www.eteach.com/International/*): This website allows you to upload your CV so that schools can find you, and offers a very friendly jobs search platform (containing thousands of international vacancies)

3. *Teaching Abroad Direct* (*http://www.teachingabroaddirect.co.uk/*): This is a very professional agency based in London that works with schools all over the world to place exceptional teachers in high quality teaching positions. Their website also has some good information about international curricula, CV writing tips and some general advice before you decide to board the plane.

Secret number 43: The world becomes smaller when you teach overseas

Thailand is proud to host many of the best international schools in the world. Standards are high and foreign teachers in this country are held in very high regard (as they are in the majority of overseas territories). However, even for a country like Thailand, which had 167 registered international schools within its borders in 2013[9], the connections between staff at different institutions are very intimate. Principals and head teachers regularly gather together for discussions and meetings, and

---

[9] International Schools Group: CIA World Factbook. (2014). [Online] Available from: http://wenr.wes.org/2014/07/the-booming-international-schools-sector/ [Accessed 1st October 2015]

expatriates who've lived in a particular country for a while tend to build up a network of educational professionals that they communicate with on a frequent basis. What are the implications of this for a new teacher, in a new country? That's simple: you need to be very careful about who you annoy, and who you befriend.

Tony had just been appointed at a leading international school in Japan as a Teacher of Mathematics. He had never taught in the international arena before, and he was really looking forward to this new adventure in his life.

Tony settled in pretty well at his new school, but he made a mistake that too many international teachers make: he thought he could take it easy and he saw this new job as a kind of 'long holiday'. Tony quickly got to know where the local bars were, and he had no trouble in spending the majority of his weekends frequenting these establishments. He began to oversleep on many a Monday morning, and he would frequently take days off work to recover from a hangover. The principal was not best pleased, and he called Tony into his office to tell him that he would not be renewing his one-year contract, but that he would provide him with a suitable reference so that he could move on. The principal also offered some words of advice, which centred on punctuality and attendance (Tony had, actually, been spoken to about this on two previous occasions).

Tony immediately started applying for new jobs in Japan. In some cases his application documents earned him an interview with some of the most discerning school heads in the international school circuit. However, what Tony didn't know was that there was an all-Japan international schools head's meeting taking place at around the time he was applying for jobs. At that meeting, a few of the heads mentioned that they had an applicant for a Mathematics position: Tony, and they wondered if anyone else knew him. Tony's current head knew him, and he wasted no time in telling the blatant truth about his attendance and punctuality issues. In an instant, Tony's chances of being employed by a suitable new school were reduced significantly, to the point where Tony had to go back home to the UK to find work.

I've witnessed just how small the international teaching circuit is on too many occasions whilst teaching in Bangkok. Over the past seven years I have taught in three different international schools and every time I have moved to a new school, there's always been someone there who knew the colleagues I used to work with in my previous school. Some of my former colleagues have worked up such an 'infamous' reputation that I've heard the same rumours being repeated time and time again, by different people, across a variety of settings.

Once again, we see how managing one's reputation is incredibly important when working as a teacher. People will talk about you behind your back: it's inevitable, and when you're working on the international circuit this 'shadow chatter' can either destroy you or enhance your profile. What would you like people to say about you to a prospective employer, or a new colleague of yours? Make sure that your outward actions match the ideal perception that you would like people to have of you, and your contacts will sing your praises instead of laughing about your flaws.

Secret number 44: Your problems may follow you when you fly away

If your motivation to leave your home country revolves around personal problems you have such as debt, a broken relationship or family issues, then don't assume that all of these problems are going to vanish as soon as the landing gear hits the tarmac in your new city. Certain problems, especially those concerning money, can actually be exacerbated when leave your home country. Here are my top tips for making sure that a problem at home doesn't become a nightmare abroad:

1. *Money*: Think long and carefully about any debt-related or financial issues you have, and aim to resolve them before you

board the plane. Many expatriates find it difficult to transfer funds back to their home country once they're abroad, and this can have consequences in terms of meeting credit card and bill payment dates. You must ensure that you've enquired beforehand about the ways in which you can deal with your finances abroad, and you must remember to follow through. When one is residing in a foreign country, it can be easy to forget about the financial commitments you have in your home country. In the early stages, this can manifest as an awkward message or letter from your creditor, progressing to international criminal action if the issue is not dealt with. It might be a good idea for you to leave some savings in your native bank account which you can use to pay your bills and loans in the first few months of your new adventure. You may wish to get a trusted friend or family member back home to help you with this.

2. *Relationships*: Don't burn any bridges before you fly away. You may be travelling to an exotic new country to start a wonderful new chapter in your life, but you never know when circumstances may force you to return home to your native country. Try not to upset people before you leave, for example, by venting your pent-up grudges that you've had for years. You may also want to keep in touch with people at your old school as you may need to call upon them for advice, resources and help.

3. *Health*: Try to bring all of your medical records with you when you travel, and have them deposited at the hospital you plan to use when you start at your new school. Whilst medical care provided overseas can be of an extremely high quality (especially when your school pays for private medical insurance as part of your package), it can be very difficult for doctors to suggest a suitable course of treatment if your exact medical history is unknown. If you end up spending a great deal of time teaching overseas, then you may find yourself moving from hospital to hospital, or even country to country! It is essential that you do

not underestimate the importance of keeping your medical records safe, accessible and updated. Unfortunately, however, this is the one aspect of international teaching that is most overlooked by teachers.

4. *Crime*: If you've committed any kind of serious criminal offence in your home country, then you almost certainly will not get a job at a reputable international school overseas. Most will require you to complete a criminal records check before you leave your home country but even if your school does not require this, you must still be upfront and honest about any criminal history you have. The ramifications for you can be severe if your school finds out about it later.

5. *Online*: Clean up your online profile. Look at all of the social media channels you have, all of your blog posts, forum replies, comments and any other material you've submitted online. Also, remove anything that puts you in a bad light: international school managers are using 'internet screening' more and more often these days. Additionally, be very careful about who you connect with through social media, and never connect with current students. Whilst it's important to keep in touch with your former students, you still have to be careful about what they can read about you, or from you, online. Your former students may be connected with your current students, and they can pass on information easily. You'll also find that the student world of international teaching is just as small as the teacher world, and students in different international schools do communicate and connect with each other.

Basically, it's very simple: Clean up your 'life house' before you move out, and you're experiences overseas will be that much more pleasant.

Secret number 45: Experience is essential

Demand for student places at English speaking international schools, along with competition for teaching positions overseas, is increasing year after year. In fact, a very worrying set of data came out of a study by International School Consultancy (ISC) Research for the 2014 – 2015 academic year. The study found that about 18.000 teachers left the UK to teach at international schools in overseas territories. The alarming thing about this figure is that it is higher than the number of teachers who qualified through the university PGCE route for that year (17,001)[10]. Basically, this means that more teachers left the UK to teach overseas than those who qualified to become a teacher through the PGCE programme.

Mounting bureaucracy and paperwork, poor overall working conditions, relentless government interference and a high cost of living are among a number of factors causing a mass exodus of British teachers to more appealing locations around the world. This means that competition for teaching vacancies at international schools has never been higher. For this reason, you need to make sure that your profile shines like a diamond and torpedoes the competition out of the water. Here are some of my tips for ensuring that you land that dream job overseas:

1. Get some experience of teaching a range of subjects whilst you're still in your native country. International schools value the ability to teach more than one subject area.

2. Build up a strong teacher portfolio so that you have something impressive to show at interview. Keep those nice notes you receive from students at the end of the year, and file away any good examples of marking you've done, resources you've created and training certificates you've earned

---

[10] Dickens, J. (2015). *EXCLUSIVE: More teachers left to go abroad than did a PGCE.* [Online] Available from: http://schoolsweek.co.uk/exclusive-more-teachers-left-to-go-abroad-than-did-a-university-pgce/ [Accessed: 12th September 2015]

3. Take some extra courses to boost the spectrum of qualifications you have. Many universities (e.g. The Open University) offer a variety of certificate, diploma and degree courses that you can study whilst you are working.

4. Keep your current managers happy. You almost certainly will not be asked to teach a demonstration lesson as part of the interview process for a job overseas. However, what your overseas recruiters will do is exhaustively analyse your references, and will often send out detailed forms for your assigned referees to fill in. They may even speak with your principal or headmaster on the phone.

If you plan ahead and gain the necessary skills, qualifications and good rapport with your managers, then you'll have a very strong curriculum vitae that will impress any international recruiter.

Bibliography

Citations in order of appearance

- Banas, J. A., Dunbar, N., Rodriguez, D., and Liu, S. (2011). *A review of humor in education settings: Four decades of research.* Communication Education, 60 (1), p.115-144.

- Wang, S. (2011) *Under the Influence: How the Group Changes What We Think.* The Wall Street Journal. [Online] Available from: http://www.wsj.com/articles/SB1000142405274870443600457629896216592 5364 [Accessed: 17th July 2015]

- Rogers, L. (2008) Institute of Education, University of London. *Rewards Work Better Than Punishments Experts Say.* [Online] Available from: http://www.ioe.ac.uk/newsevents/21864.html [Accessed: 17th July 2015]

- UK DEPARTMENT FOR EDUCATION. (2014). Managing behaviour and bullying in schools case studies. Contains public sector information licensed under the Open Government Licence v3.0.

- Defence Advanced Research Projects Agency (2015) *Systems of Neuromorphic Adaptive Plastic Scalable Electronics (SyNAPSE)*. [Online] Available from: http://www.darpa.mil/program/ systems-of-neuromorphic-adaptive-plastic-scalable-electronics [Accessed: 18th October 2015]

- [1] Alan Leo R. (2012). Harvard Medical School. *Writing the Book in DNA* [Online] Available from: http://hms.harvard.edu/news/ writing-book-dna-8-16-12 [Accessed: 18th October 2015]

- Rogers, C. 2015. The Wall Street Journal. Google Sees Self-Driving Car on Road Within Five Years [Online]

- Available from: http://www.wsj.com/articles/google-sees-self-drive-car-on-road-within-five-years-1421267677 [Accessed 17th September 2015]

- Carnegie, D. (1981). *How to win friends and influence people*. New York: Pocket Books

- International Schools Group: CIA World Factbook. (2014). [Online] Available from: http://wenr.wes.org/2014/07/the-booming-international-schools-sector/ [Accessed 1st October 2015]

- Dickens, J. (2015). *EXCLUSIVE: More teachers left to go abroad than did a PGCE*. [Online] Available from: http://schoolsweek.co.uk/ exclusive-more-teachers-left-to-go-abroad-than-did-a-university-pgce/ [Accessed: 12th September 2015]

Suggested reading (websites)

Blog of Dr Olenka Bilash:

http://www.educ.ualberta.ca/staff/olenka.Bilash/best%20of%20bilash/bui ldingstudentrapport.html

Information on ways to use humour in the classroom:

http://www.nea.org/tools/52165.htm

Advanced learners tips by Alan Maley:

http://www.onestopenglish.com/methodology/ask-the-experts/methodologyquestions/methodology-teaching-at-advanced-levels/146378.article

Google Forms for Teachers: A Must Read Guide:

http://www.educatorstechnology.com/2013/08/google-forms-for-teachers-must-read.html

UK Department for Education Case Studies:

https://www.gov.uk/government/collections/managing-behaviour-and-bullying-in-schools-case-studies

---

Suggested reading (Books)

- Beere, J. (2012). *The Perfect (Ofsted) Lesson – revised and updated.* Independent Thinking Press an imprint of Crown House Publishing; Second edition.

- Call, N. (2011). *The Thinking Child: Brain-based Learning for the Foundation Stage.* Continuum; 2nd Revised edition'.

- Hook, P. and Vass, A. (2011). *Behaviour Management Pocketbook.* Teachers' Pocketbooks; 2nd Revised edition

- McGill, B. (2012). *Voice of Reason: Speaking to the Great and Good Spirit of Revolution of Mind.* Paper Lyon Publishing.

21409030R00128

Made in the USA
Columbia, SC
18 July 2018